ESCAPE the Mid-Career Doldrums

ESCAPE
the Mid-Career Doldrums

What to Do Next When You're Bored, Burned Out, Retired, or Fired

MARCIA L. WORTHING
CHARLES A. BUCK

John Wiley & Sons, Inc.

Published by John Wiley & Sons, Inc., Hoboken, New Jersey.

Published simultaneously in Canada.

Limit of Liability/Disclaimer of Warranty: While the publisher and author have used their best efforts in preparing this book, they make no representations or warranties with respect to the accuracy or completeness of the contents of this book and specifically disclaim any implied warranties of merchantability or fitness for a particular purpose. No warranty may be created or extended by sales representatives or written sales materials. The advice and strategies contained herein may not be suitable for your situation. You should consult with a professional where appropriate. Neither the publisher nor author shall be liable for any loss of profit or any other commercial damages, including but not limited to special, incidental, consequential, or other damages.

For general information on our other products and services or for technical support, please contact our Customer Care Department within the United States at (800) 762-2974, outside the United States at (317) 572-3993 or fax (317) 572-4002.

Wiley also publishes its books in a variety of electronic formats. Some content that appears in print may not be available in electronic books. For more information about Wiley products, visit our web site at www.wiley.com.

Library of Congress Cataloging-in-Publication Data:

Worthing, Marcia L., 1943–
   Escape the mid-career doldrums : what to do next when you're bored, burned out, retired or fired / Marcia Worthing, Charles A. Buck.
      p. cm.
   ISBN 978-0-470-11515-2 (pbk.)
   1.   Career changes. 2.   Vocational guidance. 3.   Mid-career. 4.   Occupational mobility.
I.   Buck, Charles A., 1942–   II.   Title.
   HF5384.W67 2008
   650.14—dc22

                                                                                    2007021313

Printed in the United States of America

10 9 8 7 6 5 4 3 2 1

This book is dedicated to Ronald M. Foster, Jr.

Contents

CONTENTS

Acknowledgments

We wish to acknowledge the guidance we have received from Bruce Wexler. He has been wise and patient and has taught us a great deal about the business of writing a book. Thanks also to our editor Laurie Harting and the group at Wiley for believing in the project and for encouraging us along the way. All of the people at Mullin & Associates, starting with Keith Mullin, deserve a special thank you–for being good friends and for providing an excellent environment for practicing the art of coaching.

Personal notes from Marcia...
Charley and I have dedicated this book to Ron Foster, my late husband, who was my greatest supporter over the years and who celebrated life everyday he lived. Thank you to my wonderful family–my children, stepchildren, brothers, sisters, brothers-in-law, sisters-in-law, and all of their families. Special thanks to Chris and Geoff, who have been there every step of the way this past year. And then there are my amazing friends–you know who you are! Thank you!

Personal notes from Charley...
I especially want to thank my partner, John Murtha, for the support, enthusiasm, encouragement, patience and sound advice he has provided for this project and everything else for almost a quarter century.

This book could not have come to fruition without the interest, information and support of many including: Jason Arbuckle, Mark Arena, John Beardsley, Eli Boyajian, Judy Casey, John DeRemigis, Susan Dunrovich, Tom Fallon, Clayton Fisher, Kim Forster, Tom Forster, Joe Harney, Ron Hatcher, Richard Hersh, Patricia Houtz, Gary Karel, Tony Manning, RuthAnn Marshall, Clay Railey, and Patricia Slingluff.

Finally, both of us want to thank all of the wonderful people who we have had the privilege of coaching over the years. We have learned as much from them as they could possibly have learned from us. They have contributed to our learning the key to coaching: to ask questions and listen carefully. People know the answer to whatever is on their minds--from facing burnout to being fired. The job of a coach is to help bring out the knowledge that is inside. Being able to support people in their journeys to discover truth from within is what brings us pleasure and what motivated us to write this book. Some of their amazing stories are told in the chapters that follow. We have changed some of the names and circumstances, but the stories are based on real people and real circumstances. A special thanks to all of the people in the stories who have brought us joy and been the reason we loved going to work every day.

Introduction

While many career books exist, few focus on the challenges and opportunities facing mid-career professionals today. Given the number of mid-careerists in the workforce and their growing need for advice, we decided to embark on this project. We are excited about the possibilities for people who have been working for 20 or more years, and we want to share what we've learned about how to capitalize on these possibilities—how to exit from jobs, careers, retirement, or workstyles that have gone stale and find fresh and fulfilling options.

This book evolved, as many things do, over lunch. We have known and worked with each other for years in New York City, and one day about a year and a half ago over lunch, we began talking about a phenomenon we had both observed: Many of the professionals we were seeing in our coaching practices were unhappy with or unmotivated by their work; however, some of them had seized opportunities, revived their careers, or reinvented their professional lives. Why had this latter group thrived while the former group was struggling? The more we talked about the individuals we were counseling, the more we realized that we were on to something.

Both of us worked with a lot of people who had been fired from jobs (often as part of a corporate downsizing) or who were unhappily retired. We also had numerous clients who were bored or burned out by their jobs and careers. And, we noted the existence of many permutations of a condition we started calling Bored, Burned out, Retired, or Fired (BBRF). Some of our clients were bored by a job they had been doing too long, and their lack of interest caused them to be fired. Others burned out from the high stress level in their workplace, and they chose to retire prematurely. Still others continued to work at jobs that bored them or caused them to be stressed out, yet they didn't look at other options because they were gripped by inertia.

What excited us, though, were the ways some mid-career professionals rebounded from the BBRF doldrums. They managed to use their experiences as a catalyst for change, learning, and growth. Even people who were fired from jobs they liked eventually said that being fired was the best thing that ever happened to them. After the initial shock wore off and they moved past their disappointment and anger, they discovered that they could capitalize on their experience and expertise in new ways. For instance, some found that losing a job caused them to assess their careers honestly, and helped them understand that their work passions resided elsewhere.

When we talked about these subjects during lunch, we realized we had something to offer mid-career professionals. Actually, we found we had a number of things to offer: inspiring and instructive stories about a wide range of people who had experienced BBRF; advice based on years of working with mid-career professionals; insight into the particular nature of mid-career crises and opportunities. We feel these insights will be particularly useful for readers, since a great deal of misinformation and misconceptions exist about what takes place at mid-career. We want to communicate that being downsized at age 55 doesn't have to be the end of a career; that some professionals make more money and find greater satisfaction in their second or third careers; that retirement doesn't have to be a time of sitting around the house, but could combine fulfilling part-time work with meaningful volunteer activities.

For these reasons, we've written this book. Now let us tell you a little about ourselves so you know that we've walked the talk.

OUR MID-CAREER MISSTEPS AND EPIPHANIES

Though the following pages will make relatively few mentions of our own work experiences, we decided it was only fair to communicate our backgrounds as well as the changes that took place in our lives at mid-career. We hope this provides us with some credibility in your eyes and also conveys that this is a topic we understand personally as well as professionally. With this intent in mind, here are our stories.

MARCIA

I spent the first 27 years of my career at Avon Products in New York, retiring in 1998 as Senior Vice President of Human Resources and Corporate Affairs. My career at Avon was rewarding. Not only is it a great company that provides women with all types of employment and advancement opportunities (something that is very important to me), but Avon also gave me the chance to travel throughout the world while meeting and working with wonderful people. Shortly after leaving Avon, I joined Mullin & Associates, a New York outplacement and executive coaching firm that offers individualized, one-on-one counseling. There, I coached and advised people from all industries who had lost their jobs, focusing on individuals hoping to transition into new fields or who want to reinvent their lives. This too was an excellent job. In addition, I'm on several not-for-profit boards, including the Institute for Women's Policy Research and The Institute for Global Ethics.

As of this writing, I am making a third major change: returning to the Columbia School of Social Work as a full-time student. Having spent my entire career in business, becoming a social worker may seem like a stretch, but it's the type of stretch that many mid-career professionals are making.

I decided to leave Mullin and obtain a degree in social work after doing much thinking—not just ordinary thinking, mind you, but sustained questioning, information gathering, and reflection. I thought long and hard about what was important to me at this stage in my life, about what made me happy. My epiphany was that I loved working with people and helping them find the truth in their lives. My thought process also revealed I wasn't growing as much as I wanted in my job; I still had a lot to learn about human behavior, and this was the time in my life to make a real difference. Though I recognized I was making a difference in the lives of my coaching clients, I wanted more. I wanted to see if I could help others in new ways—with their personal relationships, their emotional challenges, and so on. Social work seemed to meet all the criteria.

When I left my house the morning of student orientation, though, I had my doubts and fears. Had I made the right decision? What would the other students think of having someone like me in class—someone who was 30 or 35 years older than the rest of them? As it turned out, no one cared much about my age. Very quickly, the age difference melted away as we asked and answered the same questions: Why did you choose Columbia? What do you want to do when you graduate? Of course, no one knew specifically what they wanted to do, including me.

Nonetheless, I was sure I was in the right place. I had the same confidence in what I was doing that I saw in other mid-career professionals I had coached and who had undergone similarly major transitions. It brought to mind the wonderful Martin Luther King quote, "Faith is taking the first step even when you don't see the whole staircase."

CHARLEY

My first significant job was at advertising agency Doyle Dane Bernbach (DDB), starting out in what was then called the Personnel Department, and staying there for more than 10 years in Human Resources, becoming a vice president at age 30 and eventually assuming responsibility for all account services administration. It was a good, rewarding job at a major advertising agency, but eventually I became bored. I wanted a more significant challenge and found it with a start-up, a small marketing consulting firm. I left DDB and helped this new firm create a business plan. It eventually became very successful and I enjoyed having bottom line responsibility. A dispute with the partners led me back the ad agency business, where I received an attractive offer to become the director of administrative services for the Batten, Barton, Durstine, and Osborn (BBDO) agency. The job was a fresh challenge, including the chance to head a department with over 200 employees as well as to take on major executive responsibilities. I was there for 6 years, and again became bored as I managed myself out of having much to do. The managers I'd hired were highly competent and I was sitting at my desk wondering what to do next.

What I did was start a recruiting and coaching business, and though I enjoyed 15 mostly successful years, I reached the point at mid-career where I wanted more. This time, though, I wanted to try something that had nothing to do with human resources. My life partner (who had had a successful career in media sales) and I began researching bed and breakfasts, doing our due diligence so that if we actually acted on our impulse to open one, we would know what we were getting ourselves into. We bought an abandoned bed and breakfast on Long Island near our weekend house, and we began fixing it up. It took a great deal of work to create the type of house we envisioned, but when it was done and open for business, all our hard work paid off. We had three highly successful seasons, doing well in a business where most neophyte B&B owners failed. Ultimately, though, the grind of running a B&B got to me, and we sold the property. After the sale, I decided to return to consulting, but not as a recruiter, which had been my bread and butter. This time, I was passionate about coaching other people like myself who were struggling with transition challenges, especially mid-career executives who were asking themselves, "What next?"

The major theme of my story is that we receive numerous second chances in our careers, and to capitalize on them requires more than blind luck. I care deeply about helping others make the most of their second chances at mid-career, and this book gives me a way to communicate what I've learned both as a coach and as a repeat second-chancer.

GETTING PAST THE DOLDRUMS

We hope this book gets you out of the doldrums, which the dictionary defines as a "sluggish state in which something fails to develop or improve." Many mid-career professionals become stuck. Fired or retired, bored or burned out, they believe that their careers are essentially over (even if they're still working). They become defeatist and fatalistic or cynical and angry, but the end result is inertia. In other words, they lack the initiative and energy to leave a job they dislike or look for a new career. They feel like they're in limbo and don't know how to get out or lack the drive to do so.

If this describes your state, this book should energize you in a number of different ways. It offers you information and advice that should help you:

- Become aware if something isn't right. Inertia, which Webster defines as "a tendency to remain in a fixed condition without change; disinclination to move or act," is common at mid-career. Inertia is frequently rationalized away by people suffering from boredom and burnout. They tell themselves that "it's only a day job," "it's the price you pay to make it in corporate America," and "everyone hates his job."

  If you learn to move away from cynical or fatalistic attitudes and toward an honest assessment of your own situation, you're in a much better position to do something about it. When you're honest with yourself, you gain the knowledge necessary to make positive changes.

Experience has taught us that people should not give up because they were fired at mid-career or feel that once they've retired, there's no turning back. Options and opportunities are plentiful at any age, but only if you're honest about what's wrong with your job or career.

- Gain the confidence to take action. Most mid-career people should be confident, since they have gained tremendous experience, expertise, and contacts over the years that place them in enviable positions to pursue all types of endeavors. The key is understanding how these advantages translate into second careers or new directions, and this book will facilitate that understanding.

- Recognize that it's never too late to start over. As you'll discover, age-related myths abound. People are absolutely convinced that no one will hire them because they're a certain age or because they don't look young and energetic enough. In reality, age and experience can be more a help than a hindrance in achieving all types of mid-career goals. More so than ever before, people are embarking on second, third, and fourth careers after age 45. While it may not have been true years ago, today our culture encourages starting over. We have seen little discrimination against those who decide to return to school later in life or who want to start their own businesses after working for someone else for 30 years.

  Of course, it takes a certain amount of chutzpah to restart a career or begin new activities at mid-career, but we trust that the information we convey will help you take a chance and pursue work, volunteer or educational activities about which you're passionate.

- Find your next career or path by looking inside. Sometimes, mid-career professionals want to make major changes but they opt for the path of least resistance — they go into consulting because they know they can make a lot of money or they decide to work for a not-for-profit because they know a number of people who made the switch from corporate jobs. They fail to escape their doldrums, though, because their choices aren't connected to who they are.

  If you're puzzled about what to do next, the answer resides inside of you. We have no doubt that if you look hard enough, you'll find a path that is right for you, that excites and motivates you, that is something at which you can excel. Through our exercises and suggestions, we'll help you with this internal search. It may take a bit of time and some creativity—and it might require you to pursue an untraditional career path or workstyle—but we believe everyone is capable of using this introspective method effectively.

AN EXAMPLE OF A GREAT MID-CAREER DOLDRUM ESCAPE

Throughout the book, we're going to offer you examples of people we know and have worked with who have found fulfilling career directions after years in one type of field or job. We hope these examples inspire you to make a change if you're ready do so, but we also are sure that they will demonstrate how to put our advice into practice. We just noted, for instance, that it's important to look inside when determining what path to pursue at mid-career. Debbie illustrates this point.

Debbie worked as a marketing director at a major consulting firm for a number of years. It was an important position within the firm, and Debbie did well, receiving a good salary and a lot of respect from her colleagues. She also worked long hours and had little time for much else besides work. However, because she was in a staff role, she wasn't on a partner track, despite her excellent performance. At first, this didn't bother her, but over time it began to grate. Why was she killing herself when her opportunity for advancement was limited? She watched partners' bonuses increase in size dramatically, while her bonuses had more moderate increases. At age 49, she started feeling burned out, and the feeling didn't go away over the next 6 months. In fact, work that she used to be excited about seemed mundane, and she lacked her usual energy and commitment. She could have stayed at the firm forever, but Debbie recognized that staying would mean being stuck in a place that no longer suited her.

Debbie had a strong relationship with her boss and decided to be open about her feelings. They had a good discussion, at the end of which they agreed on a mutual termination, which was a way for her to resign but also receive a small severance package. Debbie began pursuing jobs in the nonprofit sector, thinking that it would lead to work she would find more meaningful. She also applied for corporate jobs to cover herself in case nothing materialized in the nonprofit sector. The partners at her firm were helpful, providing her with good leads that led to a number of exploratory interviews. Still, no offers were made, and after 5 months, Debbie was anxious. Then things began to open up for her and the networking paid off. She received two offers from very different organizations: a large bank and a group that provided support for needy families. The former offer was for a marketing position similar to the one she held at the consulting firm, and the latter was to be executive director of a not-for-profit group—the latter offer was for less money.

Debbie thought long and hard about what she should do, and ultimately chose to accept the executive director position. Even though the salary was much less than she had earned before and what the bank job was offering, she recognized that she found the combination of helping others and working reasonable hours to be irresistible. Debbie had wanted to use her skills to do something that made a real difference for quite a while, and this was her chance. She also wanted to spend more time doing the many non-work activities that she so much enjoyed, and this not-for-profit position would afford her that opportunity.

As of this writing, Debbie is thriving in her new job. After little more than year, she has helped the organization grow and prosper. More significantly, she feels like she has a sense of purpose—she is valued not only by the group's board and staff members but by the needy people she helps. She also has much less stress in her life, and when she is not working, she feels like she can truly relax for the first time in years.

THE MORAL OF THE STORY...

The moral isn't that everyone should give up corporate life at mid-career and join a not-for-profit group. Instead, they should have the courage to follow their hearts as well as their heads at mid-career.

It doesn't matter whether you want to become an Internet guru, a professor of Egyptian studies, a kindergarten teacher or an entrepreneur. If you discover a true calling later in your career, you should acknowledge it as a possibility rather than a pipedream. Too often, professionals dismiss their dreams after a certain age, fearing that it's too late to turn them into reality, or that they would be foolish to forsake 25 years of building their reputation and expertise in a given field. Debbie's story teaches that you should take your dreams seriously, no matter the age at which you discover them.

Of course, you need to temper your dreams with a bit of financial reality. Many of the people we work with want to start their own businesses, devote their lives to helping others as a volunteer, or switch to part-time work. The reality, however, is that at least some of them can't afford to make these moves immediately. They don't want to dip into their savings to fund their next career or activity . . . or they don't have any savings!

Therefore, we encourage you to filter all our advice through a financial planning perspective. If you have a financial planner, use him or her to assist you. If not, figure out the answers to some basic financial questions: How much money do you need to live on annually? Do you feel this annual cost will change in the years ahead? Are there ways you can reduce your spending to make your next career stage feasible? Can you survive if you make x percent less money than you're making now? We know that you may not know all the answers to these and related questions, so we've included materials from a financial planner we know and trust (see Appendix 1) to help you assess your financial situation relative to your mid-career dreams.

Maybe you'll need to give yourself two more years before you can quit and start on something that doesn't pay as much as you're currently making. Maybe you'll have to combine two activities, doing one part-time job to make money and another that fills your life with meaning and purpose. The key, though, is taking your dream seriously. As you'll see from the stories of other mid-career professionals, just about anything is possible.

The more resources you have, the more possible your vision becomes. We're not just talking about financial resources but your accumulated knowledge, skills, and contacts. We've found that after 20 or 30 years in any field, people have accumulated a considerable amount of savvy that translates into all sorts of new and seemingly unrelated endeavors. If you're a commercial real estate executive, for example, you may not think that your background has prepared you to be an inner city high school teacher. What you'll find, however, is that dealing with tough kids is often a matter of negotiation, and you probably know how to negotiate better than most.

Be aware, too, that the advice and ideas within these pages are relevant no matter what happened in your first career. You may have been incredibly successful or achieved only modest success. You may have loved your work for 15 years and hated it the last 5, or you may have never particularly liked it but enjoyed the financial compensation you received.

It really doesn't matter. We've coached people in all these types of situations and many more in between, and we've found that the people who are best able to realize their dreams after reaching the mid-career point are those who are willing to assess their capabilities and passions accurately and objectively. Being the CEO of a Fortune 100 company doesn't guarantee similar success working for a volunteer group. Conversely, the individual who becomes an entrepreneurial wizard in this second stage of life may have only reached middle management ranks before mid-career. The keys are: identifying what will provide you with meaning and happiness, even if it's completely different from your previous career or if it seems like an odd or inappropriate activity, and being realistic about what you need to achieve your new goals.

Finally, we would urge you to think about your choices in terms of *renewal*. This is a concept that will make more sense when we return to it at the end of the book, but for now, think about how Debbie revitalized her career and reenergized herself. Many of the mid-careerists we've worked with refer to the surge of energy they experience, the sense of purpose and meaning, the greater joy they take from life, the decrease in stress, and the chance to do what they feel they were placed on earth to do. Renewal captures these feelings, and we hope that the ideas in this book will allow you to experience it.

1

The Changing World of the Mid-Career Professional

If you're like most mid-career professionals, you've probably observed numerous changes in your workplace or industry. You may be angry, confused, scared, or resigned. You may feel that the world of work is going to pass you by or that you can't keep up. That's how Brenda, a 42-year-old top advertising executive, felt when she was told by her boss, "There was a Brenda era, and now it's time for a new era."

Change has become a constant in corporate America, but it can be a change for the better rather than for the worse. In fact, many of those in their mid-career years talk about forced change as giving them the opportunity of a lifetime. As strange as it may seem, losing a job or being unhappy in retirement was the catalyst for them to pursue their dreams and make work matter again. Yes, change may make some people feel left behind and longing for the old, pre-change days. But for those who are perceptive and adaptive, change can also provide the energy necessary to capitalize on new opportunities—opportunities that can transform bad careers into good ones and good ones into great ones. That latter statement is easy to make, but it's tough for a 55-year-old to do much about it after she has been replaced by someone 20 years her junior. It's also a challenge for a middle-aged manager who feels he is stuck in a job rut and thinks he'll never get out because of his age.

The good news: We've seen many mid-career people free themselves from bad jobs and other negative work situations, discovering fulfilling careers that they had never dreamed were possible. This book is written to help people get unstuck and move on with their lives and reinvigorated careers.

We don't want to sugarcoat the changes that have distressed many of you. We do, however, want to emphasize that these changes open doors that were formerly closed. As you read, keep in mind that it's natural to view change with a certain amount of trepidation, but with time and knowledge, change can lead you in exciting new career directions and may even reveal your true calling.

The first step in the right direction is to help you understand what the changing world of work means to mid-career professionals. In this way, you can learn to avoid the common missteps in reaction to these changes as well as view them from a realistic and positive perspective. Let's start out by examining what has changed and how it's affecting people in your age range.

SIX CHALLENGING TRENDS

Change usually increases work stress and provides professionals with significant new challenges. Over the years, people have had to adapt to everything from mainframe computers to automated answering machines. They have adjusted to dips in the economy as well as the emergence of new, unexpected competitors. Then, as now, people were threatened and confused.

The difference is that back then, after people complained, they generally realized that the consequences of these changes weren't as calamitous as were first anticipated and eventually, they were able to adapt. Today, change can be more dramatic in many ways—it comes faster than ever before, and it requires people to adapt quickly and without much in the way of training. As a result, mid-career professionals may feel that their job is leaving them behind. Let's look at six general trends and their impact on job responsibilities and careers:

1. Constant Technological Breakthroughs

Every day lawyers, doctors, business executives, and other professionals enter their workplaces and read or hear about a new and improved technology and how it will improve the workplace, making it faster, more efficient, and more productive. Industries, companies, and individuals are being forced to adapt to the digital world.

For instance, many global organization employees have had to transition to managing virtual teams or conducting business through satellite conferencing or online rather than in person. They had to create strong, trusting relationships with colleagues who they see (in the flesh) less often as well as with less than perfect telephone communication skills. For people who are used to one-on-one, face-to-face communication, virtual meetings feel like a loss of interpersonal interaction. They can't read the person's body language or observe his or her facial expressions. Text messaging, excessive amounts of e-mail, automated answering services, and other electronic communications seem like a burden to many mid-career people, even as they are per-fectly natural for a younger generation. The information overload delivered by the Internet, combined with the rapidly filling cache of e-mail messages, can overwhelm professionals who are accustomed to a steady but manageable stream of data.

The phenomenon we call "the kindergarten factor" is fasci-nating to observe. Employees who grew up with computers since kindergarten relish technology. They are curious and adventuresome when presented with new and improved devices, treating them with openness and enthusiasm. Older employees have a more difficult time adapting to all this and integrating the new technology into their daily work routines. Fortunately, this is an easily solved problem when people speak up and ask for technology training or other help. We've found that when mid-career professionals ask for and receive this help, they soon embrace these changes and become comfortable with them.

2. Highly Stressful Work Environments

One reason for premature, mid-career burnout—not to mention early, stress-induced retirement—is the tremendous pressure for performance that organizations are placing on people. Increased global competition, Wall Street investor emphasis on quarterly performance, as well as rising costs and declining profit margins have all contributed to the pressure professionals feel in their jobs. They are always looking over their shoulder wondering if they will be victims of the next downsizing, and even if they survive it, will they have to do much more work since they will be doing their own jobs plus those of the employees who were fired or retired.

In these highly stressful environments, deadlines are tighter and demands are greater. Promotions are tougher to come by, not only because managerial ranks have been pruned and flattened and fewer higher level jobs exist, but because entire functions have been outsourced—the capstone position that was there for the last 30 years may now be gone.

Due to the stress, people complain that the company has lost its family atmosphere; that loyalty to employees no longer exists; that people play politics to get ahead; that teams are given impossible assignments with no way of succeeding. They say that work has ceased to be fun and they are working more and enjoying it less.

When people tell us gloom and doom stories about their companies, we remind them that as valid as their concerns are, there is a flip side to these negative environmental trends. In a restructured organization, tremendous opportunities exist for people to shape work schedules to their needs—flex time as well as work-at-home options are common. In addition, leaner companies often perform better, which means bigger bonuses and pay raises. And finally, many of these corporate cultures have loosened up as they've been restructured—dress codes have been eased, decision-making has been pushed downward, and people are promoted based more on merit than on politics.

3. Diversity Challenges

Baby boomers have been brought up to embrace diversity. What they struggle with, however, is the reality of the diversity they face every day in the workforce. As most people have come to learn, natural tensions exist between people who come from different countries, who are of different ages, and who have different backgrounds.

Older people don't relish working for a younger boss, and younger bosses are sometimes threatened by older workers. Managing the petty squabbles in teams and other groups caused by heterogeneous composition can be a hassle. Tensions between functions, especially on cross-functional teams, can be an even bigger problem.

Diversity challenges go beyond age, race, gender, and function. As organizational structures have changed and grown more complex, diversity issues have arisen between home office and the field, U.S. headquarters and foreign subsidiaries, and staff and line departments. People are no longer sure where their allegiance lies in an era of matrixed organizations and multiple or ambiguous reporting relationships.

At mid-career, many professionals feel as if their rightful place in the company has been usurped by younger people or individuals of a different gender, or even employees from another department or country. There is a sense that they are no longer in control, perhaps because their company has been acquired by a larger, overseas organization, because the new CEO decided that Finance or Technology will drive decisions, or because a new HR leader is pushing the organization to hire more women and minorities.

The upshot of these three factors may be the BBRF syndrome: some mid-career professionals are bored since they aren't favored with new, fresh assignments or given the opportunity to get ahead, and thus are locked into a job and career routine. Others burnout from being given more work than ever before and having to deal with more conflict and tension than in the past. Still others lose their jobs because they don't seem to be able to keep up technologically, or because the company is restructuring. And finally, some middle-aged people decide to retire and opt out of what they see as a confusing and chaotic environment or leave because they've been offered retirement incentives they can't refuse.

The good news is, while your company may not value the mid-career segment, others do, especially the companies that embrace knowledge management. They recognize that mid-career professionals have accumulated a huge amount of tacit knowledge that departs with them when they walk out the door. Therefore, these organizations are often open to hiring mid-career people who know how to get things done.

4. Outsourcing/Consulting

As we alluded to earlier, outsourcing has replaced entire functions at some companies. Outside consultants have also replaced some of the advisors and services that used to be found in-house. At first, outsourcing was confined to specialized areas such as payroll and manufacturing-related functions. Over time, though, everything became fair game for outsourcing. Understandably, mid-career professionals were dismayed when they saw entire departments replaced by outside firms. They also saw and continue to view outsourcing as a threat to their existence.

We encourage our clients to consider outsourcing as a way for them to capitalize on their years of experience and expertise. While working as a consultant or for a smaller, outside service firm isn't for everyone, many mid-career professionals are ideally qualified for this new career direction. Having been on the inside for years, they understand what organizations require from their suppliers. In fact, many organizations prefer hiring firms run by people who have been on the inside, knowing that they appreciate the nuances involved in how a given function operates.

Again, taking advantage of this trend rather than feeling victimized by it requires a shift in consciousness. Mid-career people may have never considered life outside of a large organization previously, and so they don't see themselves as working for or starting their own outside business. They should at least consider this opportunity, though, since they are in a good position to take advantage of it.

5. Episodic Careers

This is a subtler shift than the previous one, but it is no less significant. Increasingly, people are making huge changes in their careers. We're not referring merely to a change from working for a big company to a small one or moving from sales to operations. Instead, what we're seeing are people moving from business to social work, from banking to teaching, from being a law firm partner to opening a home remodeling business. In some instances, they're not only making a big career change once, but twice.

This trend has been fueled in part by a cultural shift in how work and careers are defined. The old notion of working for one company for life is a thing of the past. Similarly, we are no longer locked into the belief that we were born to do one thing and one thing only. We live in a time where numerous educational institutions welcome part-time, older students who want to learn new subjects, and where workshops and seminars retrain people for new careers. We've seen people who have made a great deal of money in one career decide to pursue another career that is more emotionally than financially rewarding. At the same time, we've also noted those who worked in not-for-profit professions early on, then came up with great ideas for money-making businesses and decided to pursue them. Our culture gives permission to people who want to make these significant career changes.

Given that we're living and working longer, it makes sense that this trend has taken hold. Too often, though, baby boomers are overlooking the possibilities this trend holds, in part because they can't imagine, as one of our clients put it, that "this dog can learn new tricks." People need to get past the old notion that one career defined them. They need to recognize that some people were born to do more than one thing, and sometimes even two or three things.

6. Premature Endings

People are leaving the workforce at a younger age today than in the past. Some are leaving involuntarily while others are taking advantage of sizable benefits packages. Whatever the reason, these early retirees are often highly skilled professionals who are financially secure and also possess the energy and desire to do something different.

However, the myth of retirement in our society is powerful. For years, retirement has been perceived as a goal, a nirvana of easy living and fun. As a result, people who find themselves retired at 50 or 60 think to themselves, "I'm lucky; I can afford to do nothing the rest of my life; I should relax and enjoy it." If this is the case, they should enjoy it and not feel guilty or embarrassed. Some people, though, don't want to relax. They retain the drive and ambition to pursue unrealized career goals. They like being employed, having a place to go in the morning and being around people. They have the resources to start their own business in pursuit of these goals or to go back to school to master a new body of knowledge and start over. These paths are only possible, though, if people stop dismissing them as pipedreams.

In the following chapters, we're going to examine these and other opportunities that have emerged in recent years and suggest ways to capitalize on them. For now, though, let's meet a mid-career professional who is suffering from burnout caused by the changes that have taken place in his particular field.

STUCK IN THE DOLDRUMS

Dan, 53, is a human resources manager for a large, public corporation. Throughout the company, he is known as someone who has great rapport with employees and line managers, and for years he has been the company point person when it comes to counseling employees on careers and performance issues. His empathy and insight has helped the company retain key employees as well as develop those who might otherwise have become stuck.

Dan isn't bored with his job, but he finds himself frustrated and under stress because of ongoing change—especially change involving information technologies. Every day seems to bring a new piece of software to master, a virtual meeting to attend, or the transfer of paper tasks to computerized ones. Dan has a boss who is 7 years his junior, and he is especially irritated by her love affair with the new technology and her insistence that he acquire computer skills that he currently lacks. For instance, when his boss suggests that Dan put his calendar online to facilitate scheduling, Dan resists. He tells her it feels like an invasion of his privacy; he also doesn't want to invest the time necessary to learn how to use the calendar program. Though his boss lets him slide on this issue, she insists that he attend a computer training session she recommends. Though he gives in, he resents it and tells others in his department that the training is a waste of time.

The tension between Dan and his boss escalates as they clash over one new requirement after another. Finally, Dan's boss calls him into her office and warns him that if he doesn't adapt to the changing environment his job will be in jeopardy. Dan wants to tell her he quits, but he can't afford to do so for another 5 years. As a result, he grudgingly accommodates his boss' requests, but he loses his zest for his work as well as his effectiveness. He is burned out, and he is just putting in his time until he has enough money to get out.

Think about Dan's situation for a moment before we tell you the outcome. Do you believe he was a victim of changing times? Or do you think that he was too stubborn for his own good?

Like many mid-career professionals who have enjoyed a measure of success doing things a certain way, Dan was disturbed when the changes in his environment seemed to be a hindrance rather than a help. When he protested these changes and his boss refused to be swayed, he felt as if his opinion no longer mattered. When his boss gave him an ultimatum, he felt angry and fearful. All these feelings contributed to a sense of burnout. One of the most insidious aspects of burnout is that it makes people think that the best they can hope for in a job is survival, and Dan shared this belief. As a result, he didn't even consider his options when his boss issued her threat because he didn't believe he had any. For a number of months, all Dan could do was feel sorry for himself and angry at his boss, going through the motions and displaying little of the emotional intelligence that had helped him be a strong HR person.

When we began working with Dan, it was clear that this was a talented, accomplished individual who could still thrive in a top HR job. In a burned out condition, unfortunately, people are so stressed that they fail to perceive this possibility. All they think they're capable of is getting by and then getting out.

Working with Dan, we had him do three simple things. First, we set up a few informational interviews with HR executives at other companies. Through these interviews, Dan began to grasp that just about every HR department had experienced a technological transformation, and that his situation was not unique; that his boss was not out of line when she tried to improve his technological literacy. Second, we coached Dan on the need to be flexible. We told him that he didn't need to change his values, but that if he wanted to thrive in a new organizational environment, he had to stop being so rigid in response to new policies and procedures. Third, we encouraged him to do as his boss suggested—take courses and work hard at becoming technologically proficient.

Because there was a lot of bad blood between Dan and his boss, he decided to apply for other jobs. The three actions he had taken reenergized him, and he began sending out his resume and working his extensive network of colleagues. He was soon hired by one of his employer's competitors. Though it took a few months for Dan to adapt to the new culture, he made a successful transition primarily because he did what he needed to do: become technologically proficient.

The lesson of Dan's story is that mid-career professionals must resist the feeling that their time has passed and that there's nothing they can do to remedy their burnout—or whatever negative feelings have caused them to be stuck. They should recognize that inaccurate self-perceptions are often caused by environmental changes and that they have the ability to adjust.

Whether you're 40, 50, or 60, you probably are in a good position to adapt to whatever changes are impacting your career and take advantage of them. The first step in this process, though, is to be aware if you're suffering from BBRF syndrome.

AN ASSESSMENT TOOL

All of us at some point in our careers feel bored or burned out. Many of us have been fired and some of us contemplate early retirement. None of this is unusual or harmful to our careers. It becomes harmful, however, when we respond to any or all of these factors by shutting down or sinking into a funk, especially at mid-career. At this point in our careers, we are vulnerable to cynicism and apathy. We may feel we lack the energy and optimism that we possessed in our twenties or thirties. If we're fired, we think we deserve it or that we'll never find another job. We see retirement as our only option. We can't handle the changes that our occurring in our companies, industries, and careers in general, and so we basically give up or just try to get by.

Does this sound like you? To assess whether the BBRF syndrome is affecting you and your career, answer the following questions:

1. Do you find yourself weary of dealing with new employees coming and going constantly, or that you have little in common with colleagues who are of different ages and backgrounds?

2. Do you find yourself watching the clock when you're at work and feeling like it's your worst, most boring class when you were in school; has work stopped feeling like fun at least some of the time and now really feels more like work?

3. Have you recently been fired, and are you convinced that you were fired because you're older, because you no longer fit in or because your new boss simply didn't like you or was threatened by you?

4. If you're out of work for any reason, do you believe that you'll never find another job, or that people won't hire you because of your age?

5. Are you retired or planning to retire soon even though you don't want to because retirement seems like your only option, or because you feel you are no longer valued by your company?

6. Has your demeanor at work changed in recent years? Do you find yourself snapping at people frequently or displaying impatience in some other way, are you often irritated with bosses, direct reports, or colleagues, or are you tired and lethargic in the middle of the day for no good reason?

7. Do you resist changes in processes and policies that you believe will diminish your effectiveness and prevent you from receiving a promotion or good performance review?

8. Is your professional self-esteem lower than it has been in the past, or do you believe that other, younger people are passing you by or soon will be?

9. Are you reluctant to consider any career paths besides the one that you've been on for the last 10 or 20 years?

10. Are you intimidated by the new technology, hate virtual meetings, or resist or rebel against new technological systems?

11. Has the increased stress in your job made you cynical and pessimistic? Do you frequently talk about the "good old days" and complain that your organization's leadership no longer cares about their people?

12. Do you find that you're unwilling or unable to do anything to shake yourself out of your work torpor, that you're content to just go through the motions in order to collect your paycheck, or do you avoid stretch assignments or any type of work challenges?

Assess your "yes" responses to the questions as follows:

0–3 yes responses: Unlikely to be afflicted by BBRF Syndrome

4–6 yes responses: Moderately vulnerable to BBRF Syndrome

7–9 yes responses: Likely to have BBRF Syndrome

10–12 yes responses: Mired in BBRF Syndrome

GET YOUR HEAD OUT OF THE PARADIGMS

Time and again, our clients who are suffering from mid-career malaise have work views that are mired in the past. To a certain extent, this is to be expected. After all, you were taught certain truths about work and careers, they were valid for many years, and it's only natural to assume that they still are valid. Actually, it's only natural if you don't submit these truths to some hard analysis. You're going to resist change rather than adapt to it unless you recognize the paradigms for what they are: verities from a bygone era.

Consider, therefore, the following five paradigms from the past and whether you still believe they govern your job effectiveness and career success:

1. *The most important thing is to be true to myself.* This is a noble concept, and we would encourage you to be true to deeply held beliefs and values. Some baby boomer professionals, however, use this paradigm as a justification for their myopic viewpoints. They refuse to consider a new manufacturing process or a change in business strategy because "that's not the way we do things around here." They convince themselves that it's wrong to downsize or that global expansion is the type of risk their mentors taught them to avoid. People need to be true to the values and rules of a rapidly changing marketplace, and clinging to outdated business beliefs sets you up for failure.

2. *Old dogs don't learn new tricks.* How many times have you said or thought the following: "I've been successful doing things one way for years. I'm too old to change now and learn something new." Learning is critical for everyone who wants to have a successful career. Whether you're 30 or 60 or 70, your success and happiness are dependant on how quickly you climb new learning curves. Many new kinds of information, products, services, and entertainment bombard us daily, and we must be curious about this barrage and willing to try and master it (rather than be overwhelmed). Knowledge management has become a buzz word for a reason. If you expect your old knowledge to sustain your career, you're sadly mistaken.

3. *Life is fair.* Talk to a twenty-something in your office and ask him or her if life is fair. The response will be: Are you nuts?!!? Most young people recognize that we live in a chaotic, volatile world where all their good work can be blown up in an instant. If you're a baby boomer, on the other hand, you probably were taught that if you worked hard and got results, you'd be rewarded. Certainly hard work often is rewarded. Sometimes, however, hard work and top performance are ignored. An acquisition or change of management can cause you to fall out of favor in an instant. In a fast-changing

environment, your 20 years of dedication and superior results may count for nothing. This fact shouldn't make you angry or frustrated. Instead, recognize that while organizational life may not be fair, it also offers more and faster opportunities for advancement than in the past. The stigma of being fired or changing jobs frequently has largely disappeared. One bad reference from a boss who dislikes you won't ruin your career. People are more open-minded about different work styles and more tolerant of failure. In short, you can sink fast in one environment, but whatever failures or problems you've experienced probably won't stop you from advancing in a new job or a new career. Therefore, the new paradigm is: Life isn't fair, but it is more forgiving than in the past.

4. *With experience comes wisdom.* A corollary of this paradigm is with experience comes seniority, security, and promotions. If this is your expectation, you're likely to be disappointed. In our changing world, older employees don't automatically gain respect from their juniors, and workers with seniority aren't necessarily rewarded for their experience and tenure. A significant percentage of your experiences, in fact, are irrelevant or at least tangential to the way business is done now. In a flattened organization driven by technology and teams, your years in a hierarchical structure may not be relevant. Rather than being bitter or depressed because all your experience is no longer useful, you must recognize that some of your experience certainly gives you an edge on younger people. More important, real wisdom comes to those who are agile, who can adapt to new situations and events. You will be rewarded based on your flexibility rather than your years of service.

5. *Everyone should practice the Golden Rule.* Civility and good manners are no longer the norm. In a fast-paced, high-stress environment, people don't always have time to return calls. You may have a boss or a client who speaks rudely to you because he's under deadline pressure. You may have a colleague who breaks a promise he made you or even forgets he made that promise. If you're continuously becoming angry at others who are ill-mannered or inconsiderate in their dealings with you, you're going to burnout fast. If you allow your feelings to be hurt by those who ignore the Golden Rule,

you're going to waste precious time and energy. Developing a thick skin is the new paradigm.

HOW TO PREVENT YOUR CAREER FROM BEING SIDETRACKED BY YOUR "CHANGE REACTION"

If you nodded when you were reading any of the above, join the club. A volatile work environment makes many of us say and do things that are not in the best interest of our careers. Therefore, the next time change makes you say something cynical or act pessimistically about your career, try doing the following:

• *Acknowledge and then get rid of the anger and other negative emotions.* At mid-career, people feel stuck and their emotions can lead them down a negative path. Don't get caught in this trap. It's fine to react emotionally to change, but don't wallow in it. Recognize that sustained anger or other negative emotional states will stifle your job effectiveness and career progress. Even more important, these emotions can put blinders on what can be a positive new experience—a second chance at a new job, new career, or new opportunity within your current organization.

• *Take the high road.* Some mid-career professionals react to a difficult new boss, a mediocre performance review, being downsized, a new management team, or a change in work responsibilities or policies with invective. They confront people, they complain, and they criticize. In short, they burn bridges—bridges that are often necessary to make their next career moves. As unfairly as you feel you've been treated or as stupid as a new policy may appear, work hard at maintaining relationships. Much more so than in the past, it's who you know that counts.

• *Fake it until you make it.* Many mid-career professionals we've worked with have said that they feel like they no longer fit. The new work team structure, the knowledge management initiative, the additional work load, and the new responsibilities all make people feel like novices even though they possess 20 or 30 years experience. If you appear flustered and uncertain and say you can't do it, that will be people's perceptions. If you don't make a big deal about being a learner, however, you'll probably master a new area faster than you thought possible. As a result, you'll be perceived as a quick study who can handle transitions easily.

• *Maintain your sense of humor.* This is a coping device, and you're going to need to cope with change—having a boss who is many years your junior, starting over in a new field, or moving from the for-profit to the not-for-profit sector. We've found that people who can laugh at their mistakes and their discomfort generally have an easier time emerging from mid-career doldrums.

• *Keep your options open.* Some people are obsessively myopic in their career outlooks. They refuse to consider another employer, another field, starting their own business, volunteering, or 100 other career paths beyond the one they've been on for *x* number of years. As you'll discover in the next chapter, keeping your options open means increasing the odds that you can capitalize on the opportunities that are proliferating in a changing marketplace.

2

Your Career Is in a Turnaround: A Great Environment for Fresh Starts and New Directions

If you've just found yourself out of a job, you may be skeptical that opportunities abound for mid-career professionals. We think though, that if you keep an open mind about this issue, you'll discover that more opportunities exist than ever before for someone in your position—someone with years of experience, someone with a lot to offer, and someone who can redirect his or her career in any number of new directions. Perhaps the best way to think about your emerging options and opportunities is that they are the flip side of the trends we've just discussed. Yes, organizations have downsized many mid-career people out of jobs, but as a result of their lean staffs, they need to outsource many jobs, hire more consultants, use more part-time workers, providing more work for experienced professionals who are suddenly unemployed or dissatisfied with their current situations.

Mid-career paths don't always look like they did when you were starting out. You may find a new, true calling in the most unlikely of places or positions. You may volunteer one day a week and quickly discover that you want to turn this volunteering effort into a part-time or full-time job. You may learn after 20 years working for huge corporations that you relish the chance to work for a 20-person start-up.

The best news we can give you is that more possibilities exist today for mid-career professionals than ever existed in the past. To help you consider some of these possibilities, let's begin by examining an area that offers a lot of potential to those who have experience in the corporate world: the outsourcing revolution.

A NEW WAY TO CAPITALIZE ON YOUR SKILLS

As you probably know, organizations are outsourcing every conceivable function and task. They're doing so for many reasons—labor costs are cheaper outside the United States, a highly specialized external group can handle certain responsibilities with greater speed and efficiency than internal people, organizations want to get "lean and mean" to deliver better financial results, and so on. The odds are that if you worked for a large company over the past 10 or 20 years, you've watched as your company divested itself of divisions, subsidiaries, functions, and parts of functions. While some work has been moved overseas, much of it remains in this country, albeit spread out in increments to all types of new and established companies.

The most commonly outsourced functions are accounting, benefits administration, hiring, information technology, and creative services, but there is opportunity in just about every field. We should also differentiate outsourcing from temporary agencies, the latter involving businesses that provide administrative and management people for hire on a temporary basis. Consultants form a third category, and while there can be some overlap with outsourcing providers, consultants generally focus on business strategy, leadership, or technology, and they usually offer ideas and advice rather than services.

While it's true that any professional can set up a firm to supply outsourcing services or work for suppliers, mid-career professionals are often in the best position to take advantage of this trend. If you were the CEO or vice president of a large organization, and you needed to hire someone to handle a human resources function that you formerly handled in-house, who would you select: A 28-year-old with relatively little experience, or a 48-year-old who knows the ropes? In fact, you would probably be more inclined to hire an individual who worked in an HR function at a similarly sized corporation.

Without even being aware of it, many mid-career people have unknowingly prepared themselves to provide all kinds of business services. Are you aware of how prepared you are to do so? Have you:

- Kept up a relationship with your contacts at a former employer?
- Began doing small, freelance projects for a former employer or another firm in your area of expertise?
- Made formal and informal efforts to remain in touch with former colleagues and others in your field, had semiregular lunches and meetings with people in your field, or attended industry trades shows and conferences?
- Established a web site that communicates who you are and what services you can provide?
- Set up your own office or rented office space with a firm that you've done some work for?
- Kept current with developments in your field?

You may have taken these actions for other reasons besides restarting your career. Some people maintain contacts for social purposes while others just like to keep their hand in without aspiring to return to a full-time, or even part-time career. Nonetheless, you have laid the groundwork for such a return. You are probably in an excellent position to join a small organization that provides services to companies, or even to start your own firm. With the requisite experience, expertise, contacts, and marketing skills, you may be able to generate a good deal of business if this is the direction in which you want to head.

Some of you who are burned out or bored may have decided that joining the outsourcing movement is the last thing you want to do. After all, you're sick of doing what you've done for the past 25 years. Be aware, though, that practicing your old skills and applying your expertise in a new context can be a different experience. Freed from the culture, paperwork, and politics of a large organization, you may find new challenges and excitement in using your skills. Therefore, don't rule out doing something similar to what you were doing before as an option just because your current or most recent job bored you to tears. Your skills and experience make you marketable, so keep an open mind about how you might use them in a more meaningful way.

To find outsourcing opportunities, you can turn to a number of web sites that will help you gather information about what's available to you, given your area of expertise. These web sites include: www .outsourcing.com (part of the Outsourcing Institute); www.outsourcing .org; www.getafreelancer.com; and www.outsourcing-weblog.com.

PROFITING FROM THE NOT-FOR-PROFIT MOVEMENT

While large not-for-profit organizations like the Red Cross and the United Way have been around for a long time, a wide variety of small groups have formed and grown in recent years. You can choose any topic you feel passionate about—everything from health care organizations to advocacy groups for consumers, women, and many other individuals and causes have multiplied. You can find not-for-profits that do everything from protecting the rights of animals to preserving ancient Indian traditions.

Not-for-profits have proliferated for two reasons. First, highly successful individuals have undertaken unprecedented philanthropic efforts, as exemplified by the Bill and Melinda Gates Foundation. New philanthropists are providing far more money and resources for their altruistic passions than in the past. The huge influx of money into the not-for-profit sector has meant that more jobs exist for people interested in this sector, and it also means that a greater variety of positions exist. As not-for-profits grow, they require many of the same functions as exist in corporations. They need financial people, human resources professionals, marketing specialists, communicators and so on.

Second, baby boomers have exhibited a desire to give back to their communities, to fight diseases that impact them or loved ones, save the environment, and contribute to their society in other ways. This groundswell of interest has helped create many new not-for-profits, as well as swell the ranks of existing ones.

Nonprofits also offer another advantage for many mid-career professionals: the ability to try it on before buying. Many of you who are dissatisfied in your current position but are not ready to resign can explore a variety of volunteering experiences. You may find a particular type of volunteer work or a specific cause that is truly meaningful to you, and at that point you may want to look for full-time work in it. It's also possible that by testing different volunteer positions, one will not only appeal to you, but you will appeal to this particular group and they'll offer you a full-time job. Be aware that some people harbor unrealistic expectations about not-for-profit opportunities, idealizing them to a great extent. Nonprofits are the perfect antidote to the corporate grind for some people, re-energizing them and giving them a real work mission. However, over the years a few myths have arisen about nonprofits:

- *There are no politics.* Any organization with people vying for different positions and competing for limited resources generates political game-playing. We know a number of people who have been surprised to discover that office politics exist in not-for-profit groups as well as in corporate environments.
- *Corporate knowledge and skills are always highly valued.* Not always. Some people leave IBM or GE and figure that any not-for-profit will automatically treat them as A players. In reality, some top people at not-for-profits are dismissive toward their corporate colleagues. They say to themselves or out loud, "They're about making money; we're about doing good," or "They're going to come in here and try to make us like a corporation. They won't understand."
- *It will be easy to transition to a not-for-profit.* Some professionals are cocky about the transition. They believe that if they could make it in the fast-paced world of corporate America, the more benign cultures of not-for-profits should be a breeze. In fact, they might find first that it's difficult to get hired—the hiring not-for-profit executive may believe they they'll be disruptive influences. Even if they are hired, they may struggle with an environment where results aren't measured as clearly as they are in a corporation. They may find a culture of influence rather than one of position power. They may also feel like outsiders if most of their colleagues are veteran not-for-profit people.

If you don't fall victim to these false assumptions, not-for-profit work may be exactly what you need to lift you out of your career doldrums. To determine what options and opportunities are right for you, do the following:

1. Figure out your passion. In other words, what cause or issue really compels you to take action. More specifically:

- If you could change anything in the world, what would it be; what gets you excited and makes you want to write your congressman? What causes would make you march in protest?
- If you had a million dollars and had to donate it to one charitable cause, which one would you choose?
- Are there injustices in your community or state, and do you feel sufficiently angry about them that you can see yourself working to right these wrongs?

2. Recognize that you have an almost infinite number of not-for-profits to choose from. Don't limit yourself to an organization that seems okay but isn't a good fit with your interests. You would be amazed at how many possibilities exist, no matter how esoteric your passions might be. If you love fly fishing, you might join the Federation of Fly Fishers. If you're concerned about children's diabetes, you might become involved in the Children's Diabetes Foundation. Use the Internet and other tools to explore all the alternatives until you find the right one for you.

3. Consider all the various ways in which you might become involved with a not-for-profit. Some people choose to work full-time in ways similar to their corporate positions. To get a sense of what type of jobs are available, click on www.idealist.org. Other people are more interested in volunteering, and if you Google the words, "volunteer opportunities," you'll discover a wide range of ways in which you can contribute on a part-time basis. Be aware, though, that some people we've counseled have started off as volunteers, realized how much love they working for a cause they believe in and eventually taken full-time positions. A third possibility is serving on not-for-profit boards. Obviously, strong contacts and connections make you an attractive board candidate. Board members at not-for-profits are focused on raising money, and it's to your advantage if you have a strong network into which you might tap. Still, some opportunities also exist for people with expertise in a given area; volunteer groups like board members who have state-of-the-art knowledge. Sometimes, too, people volunteer for not-for-profits, work tirelessly on their behalf, and develop an expertise in fundraising, event planning, or communications. As a result of their knowledge and dedication, they become strong candidates for other boards.

4. Determine whether you're willing to make the tradeoffs not-for-profit work demands. Are you willing to work for less money than you received in the for-profit sector? Do you believe that you'll be fine working in a smaller office, flying coach, and sacrificing other perks you enjoyed in your previous job? This isn't to say that the tradeoffs are all one sided. Most not-for-profits offer greater work schedule flexibility, not to mention the chance to fight for a cause in which you believe. Still, you should assess whether you can accommodate the loss of resources and perks that are standard at many large for profit organizations.

FLEXTIME, PART-TIME, ANY TIME: MORE STYLES TO SUIT YOUR NEEDS

We can't count the times people have come into our offices and said, "I want to work, but only part-time."

In the past, part-time work had a vaguely negative connotation, suggesting you weren't qualified enough to be hired full-time. In recent years, though, the notion of more creatively structured positions has become accepted by many organizations. Job-sharing, permanent temporaries (i.e., 20-hour-a-week permanent positions), flextime, and work-at-home arrangements have all become common.

You may be able to create the ideal second career by limiting your hours and pursuing a hobby in the remaining time. Or you may combine two or three part-time jobs for the variety. In fact, we're seeing an increasing number of people who enjoy "portfolio" careers: a combination of everything from school to volunteer activities to part-time jobs. The freedom to mix and match various jobs and interests offers some people tremendous satisfaction. These are people who may require a certain amount of income and benefits, but they also want the chance to do meaningful work and to learn new things.

Retail, health, and technology sectors have been especially receptive to part-time and alternative workstyle people. If you have strong tech skills, you can probably find an employer who values these skills sufficiently to allow you to set your own hours and work location. Nurses and other healthcare workers remain in short supply, and if you want to work at night or weekends, you can probably find a situation that meets your needs. Retailing remains a seasonal business, and both large and small stores are always looking to add people part-time during the Christmas shopping season and busy times.

You would be surprised at how many white collar professionals are taking advantage of these opportunities. Formerly high-salaried executives are becoming Starbucks baristas; former lawyers and bankers are taking jobs as Border's Books salesclerks. They're doing so for many reasons, including the prospect of health benefits offered by some companies. Others are attracted to low-stress jobs and environments—you don't work a full 40-hour week and you don't take your work home. These jobs may also offer a sense of community. Camaraderie exists among the small group of people who work in a store, and the friendships and conversations with colleagues and customers are rewarding. Third, these part-time jobs give people the chance to work at something they truly enjoy. Some people love books, others love coffee. They may have been a marketing executive for P&G in their past career, but in that position they were removed from what they were selling. In these part-time positions, people are on the front lines dealing with others that share their same interests and passions.

If you're interested in part-time work, think about the options available to you by asking yourself the following questions:

1. Is your motive for working part-time increased flexibility? Do you want to travel more? To play more tennis? Are you tired of the 9-to-5 routine and want to spend less time working and more time doing things around the house and being with your family? Do you want to have greater control over your work schedule rather than allowing it to control you?

If your answer to these questions is yes, then it might be wise to look for a job that offers you maximum flexibility rather than a specific type of work. While you might want to continue working for the money, the benefits, or the companionship, you also don't want work to dictate what you do and when you do it. Therefore, search for part-time positions that allow you at least some control over work times.

2. Are you interested in part-time jobs because they will allow you to pursue your passion? In other words, is a temporary or part-time position a means to an end? Do you want to pursue your dream of writing a novel or learning how to sail, and you need a part-time position to help fund this passion? This is fine, and we know more than one person who followed this strategy and eventually turned their passion into a career. One individual we know stepped down from a senior executive position and consulted part-time to keep a stream of money flowing in, but his real goal was to improve his golf game so he would be competitive on the senior golf circuit. After about two years of consulting and golfing, he gave up consulting entirely and joined the senior circuit.

If you're considering taking a part-time job for the benefits or money only, be sure you're doing so to support a passion rather than a mere interest. It's important to differentiate between the two, since you may be stuck working part-time in a position you find boring or even demeaning. If you're doing so for a meaningful reason, that's fine. At the same time, don't settle for mundane part-time work and rationalize it's the best you can do.

3. Are you taking a part-time job because you simply want to stay in the game and make a little money as you spend more time at play?

That's fine. If you're able to swing it financially and from a benefits standpoint, you may gain great satisfaction from focusing on play. We know middle-aged people who are doing incredible things with their play time; they're traveling all over the world, helping raise their grandchildren and becoming expert potters, painters, and woodworkers. They are finding as much learning and growth in these avocations as they experienced in their vocations. We live in a time where people are healthier than ever before and many outlets exist for older people to pursue all types of activities. This may be a perfect existence for some of you, and for others, it may be a needed sabbatical from the world of work. We know people take a few years off from full-time work to rejuvenate themselves, and then return to their careers. The pursuit of play helps them re-energize and re-enter their careers with renewed confidence and ambition.

EMERGING TRENDS, EMERGING JOBS

Emerging trends always mean new job opportunities. In the following, you'll find a list of four events or trends that you may not have considered, at least from a career perspective. Under each heading, we've created a series of statements. Circle the ones that might apply to you.

The Technology Revolution

- "I might be willing to go back to school to learn how to be a web designer, a medical technician, an online marketer…"
- "I can see myself bringing my traditional knowledge of (marketing, finance, research, HR, etc.) and using it to help a high tech company grow."
- "I can use the Internet to find job openings quickly and easily by visiting job web sites, streamlining a process that in the pre-Internet days would have consumed huge amounts of my time and energy."
- "I can network with people via web sites and e-mail and use the Internet to build relationships that will help me build my business."
- "I can start an Internet business in an area of expertise that I already have."

The Aging of the Baby Boom Generation

- "I see scores of ways to market my products or services to fellow baby boomers. I understand what they're looking for and how to communicate with them."

- "I can see myself fitting in at one of many emerging companies targeting baby boomers. I could be a valued employee of a retirement community developer, a healthcare firm, or a senior-focused travel firm."

- "I now possess real wisdom about my job and my career that I didn't have when I was younger. I can use this wisdom to be a more efficient and effective employee or independent business person."

The Downsizing of the American Workforce

- "When I was fired, the organization gave me a generous severance package. Combined with my retirement benefits and savings, I can pick and choose what I want to do in a way I couldn't earlier in my career."

- "When my company let me go, my boss and other executives said that I should call and take advantage of what they have to offer — referrals, recommendations, and resources. I have a great network that I never had before."

- "I know a number of terrific people from my company and others who were let go. We all work well together and I can see us starting a business together."

Disappearing Middle Management Jobs

- "My company eliminated my job and gave me a choice: I could transfer to another division and have the same type of job I used to have or I could set my sights higher and go through the company's leadership training program. I chose the latter, and it was the best career decision I ever made."

- "At first I was upset when my boss told me that they were consolidating his position and my position and I no longer had a job, but it forced me to rethink my entire career and I realized that I was secretly glad that I was free to explore work that had greater appeal to me."

• "I have my own business, and ever since a number of my clients flattened their organizations and trimmed the fat, I've had a surge of new assignments. I'm doing what they used to do in-house."

Most people circle at least one statement as applicable to their situation. The point of the exercise, though, is to think about change as a positive career catalyst rather than a negative career stopper. Given all the changes occurring in the legal arena, the demographic shifts and the speed at which fads come and go, opportunities exist for anyone who keeps a close eye on the social and economic land-scape. Consider how just one change—our current obsession with health and fitness—has created jobs and careers for people with a certain amount of experience, expertise, and financial resources. Specifically, here is how some people have benefited:

• Joan wrote a book on Pilates exercises for women over 50.
• John opened a "spinning"-focused health club.
• Mary became a skilled Yoga practitioner and began offering lessons to corporate executives during lunch time.
• Steve, a workout buff, used his knowledge to start a company that manufactured a new line of home gyms for people with limited space.
• Jill created a fitness web site that allows users to explore different fitness regimens best suited to their bodies, ages, and interests.

In fact, if you simply open the newspaper and read the headlines, you'll have a sense of where new opportunities reside. All the corporate financial scandals that resulted in the Sarbanes-Oxley legislation gave rise to a sub-category in the accounting and legal professions that specializes in related compliance issues. Even an event as horrific as 9/11 was a boon to the security industry, creating jobs where none existed before.

THE IMPORTANCE OF REEDUCATION

Formal education used to be for young people only. Today, we're seeing many mid-career professionals either returning to school or attending workshops, seminars, and other forms of instruction. In many instances, they're pursuing subjects they love and that may also lead to part-time or full-time jobs. Colleges and other groups are catering to this mid-career market. If you want to learn Internet skills, take a course to gain certification as a real estate agent, attend a workshop on how to run a bed and breakfast, or go back to school for an advanced degree, many options exist.

Perhaps just as important, our attitudes about mid-career education have changed. It is culturally accepted today to return to school or take courses or attend seminars. Some large corporations now have their own "universities," and many traditional four-year colleges now offer continuing education courses for adults. In short, the prevailing attitude is that it's smart to go back to school or take a class, no matter what your age.

This mid-career education provides pathways to new careers or revitalizes old ones. In the former instance, it provides knowledge and contacts necessary to move from one career to another, unrelated field. We know business executives who have become fishing boat captains and teachers who have become aerobics instructors. In terms of the latter, some mid-career executives go back to school part-time while employed and earn their MBAs, the degree helping them to move up a level in their organizations. Others go to training seminars or attend business-school-run development programs that provide a specialized area of knowledge critical to their advancement.

We'd like to share a story with you that illustrates these trends. Tom Snyder has spent most of his career in the security field. He has been an FBI agent, a New York City detective, and the head of security for a large midwestern company. At mid-career, Tom was at a crossroads, and considered a number of security-related positions. During this time, Tom decided to move from the Northeast and purchased a home in Miami. Surprisingly, perhaps, Tom discovered he derived great satisfaction out of the home selling and buying process. He was especially interested in the home appraiser's job, since it required many of the skills he used in his security positions—the ability to assess situations, be decisive, and communicate credibly. Tom is now studying to be a certified real estate appraiser at a community college, with the goal of opening his own real estate appraisal business in three years.

CROSSING BOUNDARIES, EXPLORING NEW OPTIONS

Though we've alluded to the following point, we want to emphasize it here: Many mid-career options exist today because people have different attitudes about everything from retirement to careers. It was not so long ago that most people endorsed the idea of retiring at age 65. More than that, they viewed retirement as this idyllic time in which they had no work responsibilities and were free to do whatever they pleased.

This attitude has changed dramatically. People are routinely working past age 65, and they are adding real value to all types of organizations. At a time when knowledge management has gained such prominence, it makes sense to keep on board the people with the most knowledge. While some people still look forward to receiving a gold watch and golfing, traveling, and pursuing hobbies, a much larger percentage of retirees than in the past are retired in name only. They are starting businesses, doing part-time consulting work, and volunteering. This change has been made possible, in large part, by a shift in attitudes. They and their employers and clients are age-blind—they don't believe that once you hit 65, you lose your ability or desire to contribute.

Similarly, few people today feel that they must limit themselves to one career. Many middle-aged individuals are working with coaches and other advisors and determining they want to make a switch. They don't see the obstacles to these switches that people saw in the past. They don't believe that just because they spent the last 20 years in finance, they can't make a transition to marketing. Or they determine that they want to make a more dramatic switch: from a career in business to one in teaching. People are prepared to take the knowledge and skills they acquired in their first career and transfer at least some of that wisdom to their second career.

Rachel, for instance, was the vice president of operations at a manufacturing company. When she lost her job at mid-career, she decided she no longer wished to remain in the corporate America environment, and that she wanted to spend more time with her family and work in her garden. Rachel had a hobby that she loved—reflexology (therapeutic massaging of feet)—and she decided to become certified. At first, she didn't see it as a new career. After a while though, she began contracting with others to provide this service, and before Rachel knew it, she had a thriving small business. She developed a marketing plan, began networking with podiatrists, health spas, and women's organizations and soon had a growing private practice as well as a great deal of spa work. She is currently expanding the business into nutrition counseling and is taking a course to become certified in this related specialty.

ASK YOURSELF IF YOU'RE BEING OPPORTUNISTIC

As you read about the various opportunities available to mid-career people, you may have asked yourself questions about whether you have taken advantage of them or if you're in a good position to do so. Here is a formal list of questions in that regard. We realize you may not know the answers yet, but now is a good time to start thinking about them:

1. Do you know anyone who is providing companies with outsourced services in your area of expertise? If they were to ask you to join them, would you find that job more challenging and rewarding than the one you currently have? Do you believe you have the skills and contacts necessary to start a company on your own?

2. Have you ever worked on volunteer projects? If so, do you enjoy them and find the experience meaningful? Do your knowledge and skills translate into not-for-profit work? Is there a particular cause or not-for-profit agency that you would enjoy working for?

3. Do you pay attention to the trends and events in your industry and in society in general, and think about how that might impact your career? Do you see any specific economic, technological or cultural trends that might provide you with a career opportunity, either related to what you do now or in another field?

4. Are there courses, seminars, workshops or advanced degrees that interest you? Have you thought about how taking a particular course or gaining a degree might further your career goals? Is there a new career goal unrelated to your current occupation that you would like to pursue, and if so, what additional education might you need?

5. Are your attitudes about retirement and careers helping or hindering you? Have you always thought you wanted to retire at 65? Have you always thought it was a pipedream to seek a job or work situation very different from the one you've had all your adult life? Have you seriously explored the possibility of working past a certain age or transitioning to a new career?

3

What You Do Next Doesn't Depend on What You Did Before: Moving Past the Career Myths

Mid-career people are vulnerable to mid-career myths. When you've been treated poorly by an employer, when you've been passed over for a promotion in favor of someone ten years your junior, or when you find yourself bored out of your mind by a job you could do in your sleep, you often don't think clearly about your career. As a result, you may jump to the wrong conclusions about what your future holds. It's very easy to fall victim to common career myths in these situations. They offer easy explanations for what happened. If you're feeling depressed, they dovetail with your world view.

Recognize, however, that these myths may be the very things causing you to be stuck. If you believe you're too old for anyone to give you another shot, then you've created a self-fulfilling prophecy. We've seen people in their forties, fifties, sixties, and seventies achieve remarkable job and career goals. It's all a matter of dealing with reality rather than the fears and rumors that feed myths.

At the same time, we understand that many of these career myths start out as small truths and become distorted over time. We know that it's tough for someone over 55 to obtain a six-figure income job with a large corporation simliar to the position he or she lost in a downsizing. It's a myth, however, that people over 55 *never* get these jobs, or that they don't find alternative employment that is even more satisfying, and sometimes more lucrative, than their previous positions.

The way to escape the hold these myths have on you and your career is to understand them, recognize the realities, and take actions that aren't governed by misconceptions and fears. Let's look at the seven most common mid-career myths and what you can do about them.

MYTH #1: I DID SOMETHING WRONG, AND THAT'S WHY I LOST MY JOB

When you're young and you lose a job, you are generally sufficiently resilient to bounce back and find another one. You tell yourself that you were fired because your boss was out to get you, or because of the economy, or because you were low paid and easily replaceable. When you're at mid-career, though, you may find yourself almost unconsciously blaming yourself for career or job problems that aren't your fault. Here are the self-blame refrains we hear from our clients after they're fired, passed over for a promotion or shunted off to the side in some other way:

- "If they thought I was good, they would have found another job for me."
- "I should have seen it coming."
- "I could have prevented this from happening."

No doubt, some people are fired because they performed poorly. We've found, however, that the vast majority of individuals who have performed well until they hit the mid-career wall are victims of circumstances beyond their control. They don't suddenly become lazy or incompetent. However, many people often make false assumptions about why a negative career event takes place. Let's say a 54-year-old individual is fired, and during his exit interview his boss or the human resources person tells him that they appreciate his 15 years of service to the company, but that they're cutting back and they have had to make some difficult decisions about people. He never receives a clear explanation why he—as opposed to someone else—has been let go. Thus, he supplies a mythical reason: "I did something wrong." Maybe his last performance review wasn't great. Maybe he missed a deadline for a project. Whatever negative event occurred, he illogically assumes it was the cause for his dismissal. In many instances, the real culprit was one of the following:

- Politics—he got on the wrong side of someone with influence or was on the wrong team or didn't have a mentor watching out for him.
- Economics—the company had to eliminate 10 percent of the workforce in an across the board downsizing designed to cut expenses and satisfy investors, and this individual was just one of the unlucky ones.
- Position—the organization has decided to outsource this person's function, and there is no longer a need for the skills she brings.
- Restructuring—a new boss wants to put his own people in place, and this individual isn't one of the boss's people.

We don't want to minimize the impact of a job loss or how this event clouds people's thinking. A senior marketing executive we know was recently fired, and she was told, "You lost your job because of de-layering—it has nothing to do with you so don't take it personally."

This woman responded, "How can I not take it personally?"

Good question. At the time, losing a job feels intensely personal. No matter how your former boss explains why you're out of work, you're the one who has to explain it to your family. You're the one who has to apply for unemployment or go through the outplacement process. You're the one who has to deal with telling your friends you've retired when they know full well that you wanted to work a few more years. Even if you're not fired, being "encouraged" to retire before you're ready, seeing someone ten years your junior receiving the job you coveted, or not receiving assignments you feel you deserve can diminish your self-image.

You may tell yourself that you've lost your edge, that a younger generation possesses more creativity and energy, or that you're not as careful or diligent a worker as you once were.

What you should be doing is assessing your situation objectively and learning from it. We've seen too many talented, bright mid-career professionals become stuck because they were angry at themselves, embarrassed by what they view as their failings, or obsessed with the "unfairness of it all." To extricate yourself from the "I did something wrong" mentality and get on with your career and your life, do the following:

1. Remind yourself that high-achieving, successful people lose their jobs every day through no fault of their own. Similarly, undeserving people get promoted and young, know-it-all bosses falsely assume their older subordinates can't keep up. Repeat to yourself that "It is what it is" and move on.

2. Analyze the real reason you experienced a negative career event. Recall the four common factors listed earlier—politics, economics, position, and restructuring—and think about whether any of those caused the event. Determine if you were so bored or burned out at your job that maybe you did let some things slip. Whatever the reason, be clear about it.

3. Ask yourself what this experience has taught you. Does it mean you're tired of working for someone else and being at the mercy of politics and economics? Does it mean that you need to find work in a completely different field? Does it mean you should look for something that provides your life with greater meaning and purpose? Instead of blaming yourself for the negative event, use it as a catalyst to restart your career or find a better one.

MYTH #2: AT AGE 65, IT'S TIME TO RETIRE

Or age 55. It doesn't matter what number you have in your head as the cut off for productive work. It's an illusion. It feels real, though, because for years, people were expected to retire at age 65. Because Social Security and other "senior" programs take effect at this age, people believe that it's somehow wrong to continue working after this point. In reality, no reason exists for imposing a random age limit on work, especially at a time when people are living longer and are in much better health than in the past.

Therefore, don't stop working because you feel it's somehow presumptuous to continue to do so at your age. If your organization's management is enlightened, they put a premium on performance, not the age of the performer. They don't want to lose a valued contributor at age 58, especially in our knowledge management era where employees who possess vast amounts of institutional knowledge are almost irreplaceable.

Joe Barton offers a good example of what happens when people fall for the retirement myth. A marketing professional in his fifties, Joe accepted an early retirement package from his professional services firm employer believing it was "about time that he left the rat race to those who were younger and faster." Even though he felt he still had a lot to contribute, he saw his firm becoming younger and younger and had always promised himself that he would leave "at the top of his game." So he left. Very quickly, Joe found the long stretches of idle time physically and mentally fatiguing. Still, he thought he'd adjust to retirement if he just gave it a bit more time. He didn't. Joe loved travel, and he took a number of trips, but he used to enjoy the alternating rhythm of work and travel. Travel alone wasn't enough. Even worse, Joe found that his money was running short, and that to conserve it, he would have to travel less as he grew older. For this reason, Joe began looking for work. He was open-minded about what he might do, and this willingness to try something different resulted in a part-time marketing position with a mid-sized law firm. It was a perfect solution financially, as well as from a job satisfaction standpoint.

To avoid making the mistake Joe made (or similar ones) because of this myth, do the following:

1. If you are employed by a company with a mandatory retirement age and want to keep working, leave before you approach it and find a better situation. If your company is guilty of other forms of ageism, exit as soon as possible.

2. Determine if you're guilty of self-imposed ageism. Have you convinced yourself that you have to retire at a certain age? Do you believe you can't compete with people half your age? Are you retiring because you see your colleagues getting younger and younger? Do you really want to stop working at your company because you feel old in that culture, or do you just want to find some other type of work? Answer these questions, and then make a more informed decision about retirement.

3. If you've already retired, determine if you would prefer working full- or part-time, or if you would rather remain retired. Do you want to go back to work because of financial necessity or for the benefits? Or do you want to return because you're passionate about a given type of work and feel you have a lot left to contribute? Be aware that an emerging trend is "un-retirement." Not only are millions of people returning to the workforce after accepting early or regular retirement, but many of them are returning to their former employers. According to a *New York Times* article on the subject, a group called YourEncore consists of companies such as Boeing, Eli Lilly, National Starch and Chemical, and Procter & Gamble, specializing in hiring people who prefer phased retirement.

MYTH #3: IT MATTERS WHAT PEOPLE THINK

It really doesn't. Nonetheless, mid-career professionals frequently talk about how being downsized out of a job was humiliating. Or how they don't want to make the transition from being a corporate executive to becoming a potter because everyone will think they've lost their minds. Or how their children will react if they take a part-time job at a Starbucks. Or how if they decide to work at an animal shelter rather than taking a high-paying job in the corporate world people will see them as wasting their talents. Our clients worry that:

- "My neighbors will be talking because I lost my job."
- "My friends will feel sorry for me because I don't know what to do with my life."
- "The other parents at my child's school will think it strange when I start picking up the kids when they get out for the day."

Certainly it matters what loved ones think; they're in a position to know if you're fooling yourself or running away from what you should be doing. Making decisions based on what all your friends, colleagues, and the world in general will think, however, is likely to prevent you from pursuing your dreams.

In our earlier example, Joe Barton retired early in part because of the age retirement myth, but also because he worried that his younger colleagues would view him as someone who couldn't let go of his job and move on. He bowed to that pressure and resigned, even though he still found his job challenging and enjoyable—it remained the best job he had ever had in his career. It's worth noting that no boss or colleague spoke directly to Joe and said he was too old to do the job. In fact, Joe admitted that no one even made so much as an oblique reference about his age or withheld choice assignments because he seemed too old to handle them.

To a certain extent, Joe's fears about what people thought of him were logical. The average age of his colleagues was decreasing. He had a new boss who was 15 years his junior. Lunchtime conversations revolved around subjects such as reality TV shows and hot new bands that were of no interest to Joe. He also found it difficult to pick up on some of the jargon that accompanied his firm's technological changes, and he noticed how some of his younger colleagues naturally engaged in "techno-speak."

All of this caused Joe to put words in other people's mouths. In his mind, he heard them making negative references about his age. The lesson here is to beware of projecting your own fears. If all of Joe's colleagues did in fact view him as irrelevant, that would have made for an uncomfortable work situation. While you shouldn't make career decisions based on what other people think, neither should you subject yourself to environments that are career dead ends because of other people's prejudices. In this instance, however, Joe was operating on false assumptions.

If you want to stop worrying about what others are thinking and start pursuing your mid-career goals, here are some actions you can take:

1. Assess whether you're guilty of "magic thinking," a normal human reaction. For instance, the CEO of your company rushes past you and fails to make eye contact or acknowledge you in any way. You immediately conclude that you've done something to alienate

the CEO. In reality, he just received a call that required immediate action and all his focus was on what he needed to do right away. Your magic thinking, however, caused you to assume it was all about you. If you are feeling good about a new career choice, the people around you will feel good too. When you think they're laughing at your decision to train to be a white water rapids guide or if they are disappointed that you've given up your career as a banker in favor of volunteer work, you'll find that your magic thinking is at work.

    2. Create worse case scenarios based on what other people think. If in fact people do believe you're making a bad career decision or feel sorry for you because you've taken a "menial" part-time job, what are the real consequences? Will you lose a friend over it? Will it prevent you from achieving a career goal? Will it cause you many sleepless nights? The odds are that the consequences are insignificant, and once you articulate or write down these consequences, you'll stop being so worried about what other people think.

MYTH #4: NO ONE HIRES PEOPLE MY AGE

We would be kidding ourselves if we didn't acknowledge that age discrimination exists. More than ever before, however, trends and events are counterbalancing this discrimination. As we mentioned earlier, the emphasis on knowledge management makes it incumbent on organizations to value the people who know the most. Many times, people who have been working for longer periods of time have greater knowledge than younger employees. In addition, organizations are wary of age discrimination lawsuits. Third, in a results-driven age, organizations esteem performance above all else, and if a 48-year-old job candidate seems more likely to get results than a 30-year-old, he or she is likely to receive the offer.

    Nonetheless, you may be convinced that you're viewed as an ancient in the job marketplace—and a high-salaried ancient to boot. When you go on job interviews, you are defensive about your age. You avoid applying at certain companies because you view them as youth-oriented. You hear a story about a colleague your age who has sterling credentials but can't find a job. You may even apply for some positions you believe you're qualified for and are turned down.

All this convinces you that this myth is reality. The real reality, though, is that people *do* hire people your age as long as they're adaptable and learn new skills. To get hired, you may need to become more sophisticated technologically. You may need to start at a lower salary. You will undoubtedly work for a younger boss. You may need to work as part of a matrix team rather than within a hierarchical function. If you're open-minded and willing to learn, you have an excellent chance of being hired.

Sally Stewart, for instance, worked for a large advertising agency for more than 25 years, the last ten as a creative director. At age 52, though, Sally lost her job when her agency lost a major cosmetics account. Though she was shocked when it happened—she'd never been fired before—Sally became mired in the mid-career doldrums within a month after losing her job. Part of the problem was that she wasn't alone and misery does love company. Sally had a large group of friends and colleagues, and as she networked in order to find another job, she heard one horror story after another. One man, a former agency vice president who she had reported to at a previous job, told Sally he'd been searching for a job for three years without so much as a nibble. Another friend, a former client who had worked for a Fortune 500 company, said that she had filed an age discrimination lawsuit against a company that had made her an offer, then rescinded it on a technicality and given the job to someone 15 years younger than Sally.

The cumulative, anecdotal weight wore on Sally. When she would go on job interviews, she would pointedly ask, "What percentage of your executive staff is over 50?" When she didn't having any luck getting hired within the first few months of being out of work, Sally decided she needed to change her whole approach and attitude. She started with the first thing the job market saw from her—her outward appearance. She cut and colored her hair. She bought clothes from a trendy boutique that she thought might make her look hipper.

Still, nothing happened. Sally became convinced that she was the victim of age discrimination and that it was impossible for someone her age to find a decent job at an ad agency. Even though we told her this wasn't true, she continued to let conversations with out-of-work colleagues convince her otherwise. Articles in newspapers and magazines that focused on how downsizing and restructuring was hurting mid-career people more than anyone else reinforced this belief.

It was only a chance encounter with a former colleague at a restaurant that finally exposed the "no one will hire me" myth. The colleague, who was around Sally's age, had been hired by a local university to teach advertising, and what started as part-time work quickly became a tenure-track position. This colleague told her about a person they worked with who was five years their senior and had recently been hired by a consulting firm that specialized in helping agencies make pitches to prospective clients. Clearly, some people her age were being hired, if not by agencies then by other groups that valued people with extensive ad agency experience.

Finally, a positive anecdote—so Sally took action and she opened up her search. Instead of just looking at agencies, she applied at consulting firms, corporations, schools, and even at a trade magazine that covered the advertising business. Within three months of broadening her search, Sally received an offer to become the director of creative services for a small company, but at a salary that was more than she was making at the ad agency. The company was thrilled; they felt as if they had landed a big fish for their little pond.

If you're convinced no one will hire someone your age, try the following:

1. Create a list of the skills you've acquired over the years as well as the knowledge and experiences that make you valuable to a given organization. Place a check mark next to any skill, knowledge or experience that strikes you as particularly valuable to organizations today. The odds are these check marks will remind you that no matter what your age, you have something significant you can contribute to an employer.

2. Broaden your job search as Sally did. While one type of employer may view your age as a negative, another type may view it as a positive. In the latter case, your experience and expertise will more than offset your gray hair. Expand your search to tangential employers—schools, consultants, smaller or larger companies, online-based organizations, even companies located in different geographical areas.

3. Use your network, not just to commiserate about how tough it is for older people, but to discover where people your age and with your expertise are finding work. After 25 years or more in the workforce, you have probably accumulated numerous contacts that will facilitate your job search.

MYTH #5: I'VE HAD MY CAREER, I CAN'T HAVE ANOTHER ONE

In many ways, this is the biggest myth of all. People somehow get it in their heads that they are not entitled to a second career or a fresh start at a different organization. They convince themselves that they've had their shot. If they must return to work for financial reasons, they're willing to settle for anything and consider themselves lucky.

People subscribe to this myth in part because of our youth-oriented culture and the media messages that reinforce it. More significantly, though, they recall their parents' generation and how one-person, one-career was the norm. It no longer is. Today, a growing number of people have two or three careers. They frequently move from one company to the next regularly. People who have been in the business world for 20 years go back to school and become lawyers because the law has always been their passion. People who have been in social services professions get their MBAs because they want to do well in another arena. Vice presidents are fired from large corporations, take some time off, and come back to a smaller company more energized and driven.

Though we emphasize these points with our clients, many of them are difficult to convince that they deserve and will receive second chances. Instead, they make excuses to themselves about why they're stuck. See if any of the following are familiar to you:

- ❏ I've spent my life with Company A. Whatever I'm going to achieve, I achieved there.
- ❏ I don't have the energy to start over at a new company.
- ❏ I have enough money saved up, I might as well retire.
- ❏ Even if I got a job I wanted, I don't have enough time to achieve any real success in it.
- ❏ I'd love to do volunteer work, but I don't have any expertise or experience in that area.
- ❏ I've dreamed about turning my hobby into a business for a long time, but now that I have the time, I realize that it's too scary to try at this point in my life.
- ❏ I know someone who tried a second career, and he failed miserably. I don't need any more failure in my career.
- ❏ It's better to play it safe with this job that bores me to tears than to risk trying something different.
- ❏ I've been fired once, I don't want to be fired again.
- ❏ To do what I really want, I'd have to go back to school, and that's ridiculous at my age.

If you found yourself making check marks next to any of the items in this list, consider the story of Marianne. An executive secretary with a Fortune 500 company, Marianne was stuck. She had enjoyed her work as an executive secretary, but when her boss lost his job, she lost hers. The company did keep her on, but they moved her into a lower level and told her she could stay there until she retired in a few years. This might have seemed generous to some, but Marianne missed the challenges and status of working at the company's top level. A series of events conspired to cause her to become depressed. First, she gained a good deal of weight. Second, she lived alone and her apartment needed repairs that she could not make herself and she didn't think she could afford given her uncertain job situation. The last straw was when her beloved dog died. Up until that point, she had been content to slog away at a job she didn't like and wait for retirement. Marianne felt that she had a number of terrific years in her executive secretary position, and that there was no way she was ever going to find happiness in a job again.

After her dog died, though, she said to herself, "That's it. I don't want to live the rest of my life this way." Within 6 months, she lost 60 pounds by exercising regularly and going on the Jennie Craig diet. She adopted a new dog. She took art courses at a local college and had the work done in her apartment—something she realized she could readily afford after getting her head in a better place. Marianne also met with a financial planner, and together they crafted a retirement plan that included some part-time work for financial reasons, but also volunteer work she had been eager to become involved in, plus more art classes. Most recently, she has acted on a life-long dream to write a book about her experience as a volunteer in veteran's clubs when she first moved to New York 35 years ago. In this way, Marianne cobbled together a second career that was very different from her first one, but just as satisfying.

If you're telling yourself that you've had your career and can't have a second one (or a third or a fourth), try these tactics:

1. *Get yourself in good physical shape.* Many of our clients are like Marianne; they lose their jobs or their career hopes and become overweight and depressed. While physical activity isn't necessarily a cure for clinical depression, it can work wonders on your self image. Mid-career professionals often feel enervated and pessimistic because they've stopped exercising. They struggle to climb the stairs and tell themselves if they can't do something as simple as that, how are they going to find the drive to restart their careers. Join a club or gym close to where you live. Hire a personal trainer for a month to jump-start your exercise regimen. Check out the web site www.walkstyles.com to take the easiest step in the direction of exercise—it has everything you need to know about walking.

2. *Take classes, attend conferences, or sign up for private instruction.* In other words, educate yourself for whatever career path or passion you want to follow. It's possible that you have a good idea what you want to do next, but you need to gather more information,

obtain a degree or make contacts before you're ready to do it. Don't be put off by the idea of going back to school "at your age." You'll be surprised to discover other baby boomers and older people in classes with you. It has become acceptable and admirable for individuals approaching retirement age or already retired to go back to school, either simply because they want to learn, or because the learning will facilitate their careers. It may be that you just need to take a single class to gain certification in an area; you may want to become a scuba dive instructor or obtain your pilot's license. You may be interested in taking a nonacademic course, such as to become a licensed real estate agent. Or you may want to go back to school and obtain an advanced degree in an area that's different from the degree you needed for your first career. Or it's possible that you must become more technologically proficient to compete in your current career. Whatever learning you choose, be aware that it's never too late to learn.

3. *Test market an alternative job or career.* We've found that sometimes it helps to test the waters before you restart your career or move in a new direction. Test marketing is simply a way to get a taste of a new field, determine if you're ready to un-retire, or explore other options. When you keep an idea for a new career lodged in your mind, it's sometimes difficult to give it the credence it deserves. When you translate that idea into a job, though, it seems more feasible. Test marketing may mean taking baby steps in your new direction. You don't have to un-retire immediately and take a full-time job; you can find a part-time job and see what it's like to be back at work in a different situation. If you're considering opening your own store, you might volunteer at someone else's retail establishment and experience what the environment is like. If you're interested in returning to the corporate world, you might try part-time consulting or temping to determine if this is really what you want to do. What we would not recommend is quitting your job on the spot and the next day buying a charter boat and becoming a deep-sea fishing guide with no previous experience. We're exaggerating, of course, but 180 degree instant career shifts are tough to navigate. People are often disappointed when they see how steep the learning curve is or how

foreign the work environment seems. This is when people succumb to the myth that they don't deserve a second shot at a career.

MYTH #6: CORPORATE SKILLS DON'T TRANSLATE TO ENTREPRENEURIAL OR NOT-FOR-PROFIT VENTURES

A significant percentage of the people we work with want to do something different in order to escape their mid-career doldrums. As a result, they're looking at fields or businesses for which they lack directly applicable experience. Lawyers want to run for local political office, business executives want to open antiques shops, bankers want to do volunteer work, and CEOs want to pursue their hobbies and turn them into careers. What stops these individuals from following their interests and instincts, however, is this myth. They convince themselves that they're not qualified for a job or business that they're passionate about.

That's a shame. Many times, mid-career professionals are eminently qualified for all sorts of different careers but they don't see how their management and leadership skills translate into running a restaurant, for instance. We've found that people who work for years in positions of corporate responsibility often develop a diverse skill set beyond their functional expertise. They know how to work effectively with different types of people, they're astute about budgets, they are good problem-solvers, and they understand the art of negotiation, motivation, and consensus-building. All these traits are attributes in a variety of endeavors. Certainly, you may need to take some classes or do an apprenticeship to gain knowledge about a new field or type of business. You may experience some on-the-job learning until you feel you're up to speed.

We've found, though, that when mid-career people are passionate about a hobby or contributing to a good cause, their commitment and energy often carry them over the rough spots. Some of the happiest mid-career professionals we know have retired into their hobbies. They love applying their business skills to a hobby that they're been involved with for years and now have a chance to turn into a full or part-time business. Many times, what helps them succeed in this quest is their business smarts. They don't make the mistakes that neophytes make. They are conservative in their forecasts and realistic about how the business might grow.

If you want to overcome this myth, try the following:

1. Make two lists: the first should contain your major areas of knowledge and skills from your first career, and the second should contain the knowledge and skills you believe will be necessary in your hobby-business or working in the not-for-profit sector.

2. Identify the matches between the two lists.

3. Identify the gaps between the two lists—areas where you lack the skills or knowledge you need to be successful.

4. Create a plan to fill in these gaps—taking a class, online learning, going back to school for a period of time, an apprentice-ship, on-the-job learning, etc.

In this way, you can go into a new, foreign-seeming business or volunteer position with more confidence in your abilities and experi-ence, increasing the odds that you'll make a successful transition.

MYTH # 7: CAREER SUCCESS CAN ONLY BE DEFINED ONE WAY

Some of you may find that you can restart your career in the middle by simply finding a great new job similar to the one you previously had. Maybe when you un-retire or rebound from being fired, you are able to land a job similar to your old one but with a better boss, bet-ter salary, and better environment. That's terrific, and if it happens, you won't encounter what we define as the "narrow success defini-tion myth."

Think about the common terms used to define professional suc-cess: salary, perks, job title, company reputation. These are perfectly acceptable terms, but they provide only one of many definitions, especially for mid-career people. Here are some other definitions:

- Success is turning a hobby you love into a small, marginally profitable business.
- Success is going back to school in order to enter a profession that you've always dreamed about being in but couldn't afford earlier in your life.
- Success is retirement plus putting in a certain amount of time volunteering for a cause you feel strongly about.
- Success is using your corporate knowledge and skills in a full-time, not-for-profit position.
- Success is working for yourself rather than for someone else.

Don't believe for a second you've failed at mid-career because you work for a small company no one has heard about, you make less money than you did earlier in your career, or you are only working part-time. As long as you're okay financially and have the benefits you and your family need, then you should feel free to redefine what success means to you. In this way, you'll escape the hold this last myth has on many mid-career professionals.

4

Assess the Underlying Cause of Your Boredom, Burnout, Retirement, or Firing

Many people feel down or alienated at mid-career, but they're not able to articulate exactly why they're in this state. Or they may attribute their malaise to a false cause—their age, their conviction that no one will ever hire them again, their inability to survive in a new, cutthroat work environment. Or they may believe a single event—such as being fired—has destroyed their career forever.

There are 101 reasons people cite for their mid-career blahs, and many times, they're inaccurate or tangential to the real cause. To escape mid-career doldrums, however, you need to view the cause accurately. Only when you understand exactly why you're bored, burned out, retired, or fired can you respond to these conditions effectively. To that end, we're going to help you assess each of the four areas and determine how any or all four of them have impacted your career view. First, though, we want to help you figure out if you're suffering from a more general mid-career mood disorder we refer to as Things Used to Be Better (TUBB) syndrome.

STUCK IN THE TUBB

A significant percentage of our clients are convinced that a changing workplace is responsible for their lack of job satisfaction and bleak future prospects. They complain that they are technologically deficient, that lean and mean corporate cultures don't suit them, and that their skills are no longer valued. For these reasons, they give up hope, retire, feel lethargic, and don't pursue a new job or new career.

It's important to recognize if you're afflicted by this syndrome. Of course, to a certain extent, all people over a certain age are affected by it. It's tough to get away from the fact that if you don't learn new technological skills, you'll probably be left behind. There's a difference, though, between being affected by the TUBB syndrome and being afflicted by it. While things are different than they used to be, they are both better and worse. Recognize that while certain opportunities may have disappeared, others have arisen that never existed before.

TUBB is an insidious syndrome. It's so easy for people to look back nostalgically and believe that they are victims of the current environment. This victim mentality robs people of the energy and initiative to explore all their career options. Once they become aware that they've hit the wall because of TUBB, this awareness makes it easier to snap out of it.

For instance, Melody has been a radio ad sales representative for over 20 years. In her early fifties, Melody used to loved her job; she relished the camaraderie with her ad agency clients, the glamour of the broadcasting business, the loyalty her employers displayed toward their employees, and the perks and bonuses the most effective sales reps received. Melody wasn't sure when things began to change, but she cited having gone through five mergers and acquisitions and having survived several downsizings. She found that her bosses began insisting she do more and more paperwork, they set sales goals that were unrealistic, they cut back on her expenses, and they suggested that she didn't have to spend so much time taking her clients out to lunch and could accomplish a lot more in less time if she communicated with them via phone and e-mail. Just as troubling, Melody didn't like the way the radio broadcasting industry was changing. She had relished the "individuality" of stations, how each one had a unique product to offer. Her success as a rep was due in part to her ability to match clients with just the right station and program to reach their particular audience. When many of the stations were swallowed up by conglomerates and their programming became homogenized, Melody was disillusioned. When she lost her job to a guy only two years out of college—and when she was informed of this fact by a boss who was ten years younger than she was—Melody became a TUBB syndrome victim.

For two years, Melody made only token efforts to get another job. She rationalized her lack of effort in a million ways—no one will hire me, I don't really want another sales rep job—and told her friends that she thought she could squeak by on her savings until social security kicked in. Melody complained bitterly that her industry had "gone to hell in a handbasket" and that her career was over.

Unhappy and unmotivated, Melody emerged from the TUBB syndrome only when we pointed out that she was acting like she was 90 rather than 53, and that the good old days weren't necessarily as good as she remembered. As we talked, she grudgingly agreed that some aspects of her job had improved, but she was insistent that there was no place for her in the radio industry. What about another sales position in another industry, we asked her? It turned out that Melody had never even considered applying for another type of sales job because she assumed it would be more of the same. Aware that she was in TUBB, however, Melody made the effort to rise above her assumption. She didn't like to see herself as someone who feared the future, complained about the present and romanticized the past. With relatively little effort, Melody was hired as a sales rep for a large software company, and though she had to do a lot of learning in a short period of time, she loved the challenge of the job and the feeling of being on the cutting edge of another industry. She is now flourishing and effectively communicating not only by phone and e-mail, but through text messaging and podcasting.

Are you stuck in TUBB? Look at the following statements, and place a check mark next to the ones that apply to you:

- ❏ You spend a lot of time thinking and talking about the "good old days," and have convinced yourself that things are never going to be that good again.
- ❏ You feel you lack the energy and commitment to do anything more in a job than go through the motions and remember that you used to be at the center of the action in a previous job.

❑ You believe that you're a lame duck office-holder, and that there's no point trying hard because your organization will never appreciate someone like you.

❑ You tell yourself that looking at a new career or even thinking about doing something different is a pipe dream at your age.

❑ You are convinced that your skills and knowledge have deteriorated to the point that you can't compete with younger people.

❑ You find yourself resisting learning new skills or trying a different approach at work because "this is how we've always done it."

❑ You spend more time remembering your past career triumphs than planning for future career success.

❑ You believe that employers view you as past your prime and will never give you a fair chance.

❑ You are certain that what brought you success in the past will no longer bring you as great a success in the future.

❑ You dream of a second career, starting your own business or becoming involved in not-for-profit work, but don't make an effort to make the dream a reality because you missed your opportunity years ago.

Scoring

0-2 checks: Largely free of TUBB syndrome
3-5 checks: Vulnerable to TUBB-like thinking
6 or more checks: Stuck in TUBB

BORED: WHY HAVE YOU LOST INTEREST?

Some people have been bored in their jobs or careers for years, while others find it sneaks up on them almost overnight; they look around and realize that they're no longer engaged in their work or feel any loyalty to their organizations. Boredom often doesn't result in catastrophic career consequences. A high-performing executive who has earned her stripes can coast for at least a year or two on reputation alone. She may be bored out of her skull, but her previous triumphs allow her to maintain the illusion that she remains productive.

Boredom, however, is a terrible thing in a work situation. Watching the clock, deriving no satisfaction from your work, resenting every moment you have to spend away from people or activities you really are passionate about—these symptoms signal mid-career malaise, even if you are gainfully employed.

Boredom is tricky to analyze, in large part because people don't always realize how bored they are and how it's affecting their career attitudes and job performance. We'd like to share the story of one bored mid-career professional and how the lack of creativity in her job caused her to start counting down the days until retirement.

Joyce has been a fashion designer for years, employed by a well-known clothing manufacturer. She has always had a great sense of style and she was drawn to the theatricality and glamour of the business. Joyce was once considered a top talent, but in recent years her company's reputation slid, and some people criticized her designs as being "overly conservative." When her company was bought and she lost her job, she began freelancing, but it wasn't the same. She preferred being part of an organization—she missed the camaraderie and creative interplay among in-house designers. When a smaller company made her an offer, Joyce accepted, even though she knew she would have much less creative freedom in this new job. Almost from the start, Joyce felt she was "designing by numbers." Her boss insisted that she follow a formula that their research told them sold. Joyce was paid well in this position, but the money hardly compensated for the feeling that her creativity was shriveling away to nothing. She executed the designs the company expected, but she did it mindlessly. She found herself embarrassed to see her old friends at fashion shows and read her favorite fashion magazines without much enthusiasm. Not only was Joyce bored, but she was a bit depressed, and she didn't know how to deal with either feeling. It was far from the perfect ending to an exciting career.

Job boredom can be catalyzed by many events and situations, and it is one of the most common causes of the mid-career doldrums. For a number of reasons, boredom is particularly pervasive in the modern workplace. According to a *Washington Post* article (August 10, 2005) titled, "Boredom Numbs the Work World," reporter Amy Joyce quoted Curt W. Coffman of the Gallup Organization as saying, "We know that 55 percent of all U.S. employees are not engaged at work. They are basically in a holding pattern. They feel like their capabilities aren't being tapped into and utilized and therefore, they really don't have a psychological connection to the organization."

Mid-career professionals are especially vulnerable to work disengagement. They may disengage because they feel they are being given mundane assignments that they can do in their sleep. They may find themselves disconnected because they've been doing the same job for so long, they no longer are learning or being challenged. Or they may feel disengaged because the culture of their organizations has changed, and they no longer believe in the new norms and policies.

It's true that young people can be just as bored as mid-career individuals, but they are less vulnerable to the inertia and fatalism that marks the doldrums. When you're young, you can rationalize boredom as "paying your dues" and put up with it, at least for a while. Young professionals also are better able to flee from the boredom since they usually have fewer financial and familial responsibilities: They get bored, and then they get a new job.

At mid-career, though, boredom has a more insidious effect. When we're bored at 50, we feel as if our career has gone terribly wrong. When we've been engaged and committed to challenging work for the past 20 years and boredom sets in, we feel cheated. It's as if all the years we've put in at a job has earned us the right not to be bored. It can be a devastating experience to no longer feel excited by what you do or to feel you're not an integral part of an organization. That's when the doldrums set in.

It's useful to identify the specific cause of your boredom. It usually just takes a bit of reflection to figure it out, focusing on the point in time when your job or career went from stimulating to ordinary. Why are you experiencing job or career boredom? See which of the following reasons apply to you:

- *Lack of intellectual challenge.* You feel you've learned all there is to learn in your job, and you're repeating job tasks that you've done for years. You are locked into an easy and repetitive routine, and it seems as if there's no way out. You put your mind on autopilot as soon as you sit down at your desk.
- *No chance to use your creativity.* While you may still have intellectual challenge in your job, you're not allowed much latitude in how you use it. You're expected to follow certain protocols and observe certain boundaries. Thus, your creativity is stifled. When you face an intellectually challenging problem, you're prohibited from being innovative in your solution. As a result, you're bored using the same old methods.
- *A misfit between you and the job.* We've found that some people become bored because a job's requirements don't fit their personalities. For instance: You like to be on the firing line, but you have a behind-the-scenes staff job. Or, you like to think things through, and the job requires quick decisions. The lack of a fit creates restlessness and boredom; you're doing things in ways that lack excitement or feel unnatural, and you start going through the motions rather than engaging with the job.
- *The need for security.* You're working at a job because it provides you with a good salary and benefits—it pays the bills. People keep telling you, "Be thankful you have a job," and so you accept the boredom of your job as the price you must pay to avoid going without insurance or suffering serious financial difficulties.
- *Not enough to do.* Your job could be done in about half the time allotted. Though you may ask for more work, little is forthcoming. As a result, you spend half your day trying to look busy, surfing the net, or talking on the phone. While you might be engaged in your work part of the time, the rest of the day is excruciatingly dull.
- *Demoted.* At mid-career, a surprisingly large percentage of people are willing to take a demotion to stay employed. Perhaps

surprising isn't the right word, since the tradeoff of a lower-level job may be worth still having a job to many individuals. Still, the demotion often results in a position with less responsibility and challenge.

• *Continuation of a bad trend.* You may have been working at a boring job or in a boring career for years, only now at mid-career your tolerance for it is diminishing. Perhaps you joined the family business because it was expected, or maybe you took a job that you were good at but never really liked. Early on in your career, you tolerated the boredom in exchange for the money or for other reasons. Now, at mid-career, you realize that your career life expectancy is limited. You long to have an interesting career, but you've worked at a boring one for so long, you doubt it's possible to escape so you resign yourself to an uninteresting job.

It's possible that only one of the seven causes listed above is responsible for your boredom. It's likely, however, that two or more of them may be the cause. The key is being aware of why you find what you do to be a drag.

BURNED OUT: WHY ARE YOU FEELING STRESSED, ENERVATED, AND EMPTY?

At mid-career, many professionals have worked long and hard to achieve certain career goals. Even if they've achieved ambitious ones, many of these individuals come into our offices and complain about their imbalanced lives. More specifically, here are some typical comments we hear from them:

• "I've given too much to the job; I barely know my kids."
• "I've worked so many hours, I don't have a life."
• "I'm sick and tired of working so hard."
• "I haven't had a two week vacation in ten years."

The media has covered extensively the growing number of overworked, stressed out executives, especially those in middle-management positions who have either lost jobs because of corporate downsizing or fear they're about to lose their jobs. One particularly insightful article about this trend ran in *Money* magazine (Dec. 30, 2003) titled, "I Quit: Overworked Employees are Fed Up..." The article noted that more professionals are not only working longer hours than ever before, but they're fed up with the scandals that have rocked corporate America and their suspicion that high-paid organizational leaders care little about those who work for them. The article contains a fascinating chart compiled from various surveys and sources (Society for Human Resource Professionals, Monster.com, Gallup Poll, Sibson Consulting) that estimates 60 percent of workers feel pressure to work too much, 83 percent of employees want to spend more time with their families and 56 percent of workers are either somewhat or completely dissatisfied with their jobs.

We're sure that if this survey targeted only mid-career professionals, these numbers would be even higher. This certainty is based not only on our experiences, but on logic. People's desire to work long hours, to travel extensively, and to deal with volatility and uncertainty tends to diminish with age. At mid-career, most professionals are looking for some degree of security and stability. When both are in short supply, burnout is a likely outcome for many older workers.

Let's look at some specific causes of burnout and why they are particularly harmful to mid-career professionals:

• *The perfectionist syndrome.* Some mid-career people are compelled to dot every *i* and cross every *t*. They feel if they do everything perfectly, they will have a competitive advantage over younger people who make less money than they do. While being attentive to detail and assuming responsibility for work getting done are great career traits, they can be counterproductive when taken to an extreme. If you're micromanaging your people, if you're working extremely long hours, and if you're constantly thinking about work issues (even on weekends or when you can't sleep at night), then you're inviting burnout.

• *Overworked.* This is a variation on the previous cause. You may not be a perfectionist, but your job demands more of you than you have to give. In a time when many companies are trying to run as lean and mean as they possibly can, people are being asked to take on enormous workloads. In some instances, one person is doing the job of two. You may have a Puritan work ethic pushing you to work as hard as your organization requires, not realizing it's pushing you toward burnout.

• *A combination of professional and personal stress.* Most people can handle the ordinary stress of a job, but when they are also going through a personal crisis—a divorce, the death of a loved one, a child in trouble—then the combination of stressors can be too much. One of the most common personal stress factors for baby boomers is caring for an elderly parent. Because of the relationship dynamic involving an adult child and a parent, this can often be a more conflict-laden interaction than between a parent and an adolescent child. The parent does not want to be told what to do by an adult child, and adult children often feel like they're walking on eggs. This can lead to tremendous relationship tension. It can easily push someone over the edge and make them feel that even a simple work deadline is too difficult to deal with.

• *Worry fatigue.* Mid-career professionals often spend a lot of time fretting about issues they can't control. Because they feel vulnerable, they sometimes focus on tangential matters such as office politics, rumors of downsizing, and so on. If they only worried about one thing—producing results—they would be less likely to suffer burnout. With multiple worries (some of which may be illusory), however, they invite that feeling of "too much!"

• *A failure to work smart.* This is an essential skill in cultures with tight deadlines, high expectations, and volatile environments. The people who don't burnout are those who are good at prioritizing and able to let some things go. The ones who become frazzled are those who try to get everything done and are unable to separate what's important from what's not; they work hard without working smart and end up reaping few rewards for their efforts.

• *Killer jobs.* Some people burnout because they have truly grueling jobs. They have heavy travel requirements or must deal with extraordinarily demanding clients or customers. They are working in extremely competitive industries or they're fighting for survival, and as a result, they are under constant, unrelenting stress. When you're young, you might find this type of job energizing and challenging. Twenty or thirty years later when you've been there and done that, these jobs wear you down and wear you out.

- *The boss is a jerk.* Bad bosses are probably the biggest cause of burnout at any age, but they are especially difficult for mid-career people to deal with. At this point in your career, you've accomplished certain goals and developed certain expertise. You've paid your dues, and you expect to be treated with respect. A bad boss who fails to give positive feedback and who criticizes people publicly can push you to the end of your tether, especially if she is the age of your youngest child.

Burnout, perhaps even more than boredom, is usually the result of more than one factor. To give you a sense of how this is so, consider Jennie, a high-profile feminist who is a published writer and well-known speaker. Ten years ago, she founded a not-for-profit women's rights organization. She retired after running the group with great effectiveness for seven years, certain that she had left the organization in good hands. She wanted to pursue in other goals that she couldn't achieve while working full-time, including writing a book. Unfortunately, the new executive direction didn't work out and the organization experienced serious financial problems. The organization's board asked Jennie to return, and she did so reluctantly. Today, she's under tremendous stress for many reasons: her group is competing with other women's rights groups for diminishing financial resources. Plus, Jennie doesn't have time to work on her book. On top of that, her husband has experienced health problems, and this is taking a tremendous toll on her emotionally. Jennie finds it difficult to sleep at night and feels mentally and physically tired during the day. She isn't burned out yet, but she's perilously close to that point because of a combination of factors that have come together at once.

RETIRED: WHY ARE YOU VOLUNTEERING TO LEAVE THE WORKFORCE?

Some people retire voluntarily and live happily ever after. We know mid-career professionals who are perfectly content with a life of leisure. The odds are, however, that you would not be reading this book if you're in that group. The key here is understanding what is causing your retirement unhappiness. This isn't always easy to ascertain, since the sociological and psychological issues surrounding retirement are complex. Retirement used to be a predictable event. People looked forward to retirement, usually at age 65, with great anticipation. It was viewed as a reward for a lifetime of hard work. People convinced themselves that they would have a great time when they retired, that they would have time to do everything they were too busy for when they worked.

Now, our society views retirement differently. It no longer is linked with a specific age, and in many professions it is no longer mandatory. Some people feel guilty because they're not enjoying their retirement as they think they should. Others feel like they've lost their purpose and miss the camaraderie of their work groups. Some individuals retire early from one career and then start a second one. Others are forced to take early retirement by organizations that want to replace older, higher-paid workers with younger, lower-paid employees.

Given this environment, we often enter retirement confused about what it means and what we should do. It is incredibly easy to take missteps based on false expectations and assumptions. It is also common not to understand what those missteps are and why they're making us unhappy.

To help you determine the cause of your retirement-related blues, consider the following factors and whether they apply to you:

- *Failure to think through the implications.* People often enter retirement in a blissful haze. They haven't give much serious thought to what they're going to do with their time after they've retired or what activities will give their lives a sense of purpose and meaning. Typically, they retire happily, and the first few weeks or even months seem blissful—no responsibilities, plenty of time for family, opportunities to take dream vacations. It's only later that the reality hits hard. They find themselves disillusioned, uncertain, and lacking confidence. Their jobs provided them with goals, rewards, praise, and camaraderie. When all this disappears, people need to find these positives in another way. They must understand that they are playing a new game with new rules.

Mid-career professionals talk about being blindsided by retirement—about being knocked down by the reality of an unstructured life where their work purpose has been taken away. To avoid this feeling, they need to think about the implications of this situation in advance—and make plans that make this time purposeful. This will avoid the feeling of being lost in retirement.

• *Self-deception about motives.* People aren't always honest with themselves about why they're retiring. For instance, they tell themselves that "I've had it with work," or "I'm too old to deal with all the changes," but in reality they just want to get away from a bad work situation—they don't like their new boss or the new company that has acquired their old company. They don't really want to retire, but they find it convenient to use retirement as an excuse to quit.

Self-deception is common among mid-career professionals who have been shunted aside. They are no longer on the company's high potential list, and they lack the clout they once had. Rather than recognizing that they want to retire because they no longer feel valued, they tell themselves that "I'm just not happy here and I'd be better off being retired." They would actually be better off in a situation where they're valued. Nonetheless, they expect retirement to bring happiness, only to find that it causes them to feel even less valued.

• *Mistaking activity for purpose.* You can still be unhappy in retirement even if your life is filled with activities: great trips around the world, exercising, socializing with friends, time spent with grandchildren. While the goal of improving a golf score might be sufficient for some, others require challenges and opportunities that involve skills they developed over a career. Still others want to feel that they're making a difference, that they're doing something meaningful with their time. Retiring in order to pursue travel or a hobby is fine for some, but we've found that many mid-career professionals assumed that they would derive more satisfaction than they actually do from these activities.

• *Overlooking financial realities.* Some mid-career professionals face retirement and realize they didn't analyze the financial ramifications accurately. As a result, they can't do everything they planned on doing after retiring. Or they may find that they need to work to obtain health insurance. Or they may suffer a financial setback that makes it difficult to make ends meet without returning to the workforce. In these instances, people feel that they've somehow failed at retirement. Not only are they disappointed that they can't do everything they wanted to do, but they may have to take a part-time job they don't particularly like to pay the bills.

• *Refusing to recognize that they need work.* What some people really need is a challenging, demanding job. Too often, people retire from jobs after having been under a great deal of work stress, and they're convinced that the last thing they ever want to do is rejoin the workforce. These individuals, however, possess enormous drive that doesn't diminish at mid-career. They require ambitious goals and deadline pressures or they don't feel fully alive.

If you're still searching for the cause of your retirement unhappiness, you may be suffering from an imbalance between work and leisure activities. Merrill Lynch conducted "The New Retirement Survey" in 2005, concluding that standard retirement planning models fail to take into consideration baby boomer plans and goals. As a result, some baby boomers find themselves in unhappy or unsatisfying retirements. One of the more compelling results of the survey revealed that most baby boomers don't want a retirement of full-time leisure or full-time work. Specifically, 42 percent wanted to cycle between work and leisure activities, 16 percent intended to pursue part-time work, and 13 percent saw retirement as a chance to start their own businesses. Only 6 percent wanted to work full-time and 17 percent said they hoped they never had to "work for pay" again.

What this survey suggests is that people need to strike the proper balance between work and leisure in retirement (and between volunteering, spending time with grandchildren, and pursuing a hobby as well). We've found that the balance is different for everyone. You may be someone who wants to spend 30 percent of your time working, 30 percent taking classes, and 40 percent volunteering. Someone else may want to be working 50 percent of the time and spending the other 50 percent reading and working in the garden.

The key is being honest with yourself about the balance that works for you. You're probably going to need to experiment and tinker with this balance once you retire; it's difficult to figure out the right percentage of work and leisure by simply assigning that percentage in your mind. Once you're retired and implement your retirement plan, you may find that you're working too much . . . or too little. Be adaptable in these instances. Be willing to adjust the balance, even if it means finding a new part-time job that requires less of your time, or looking for a volunteer activity that demands more from you.

FIRED: WHAT WAS THE REAL REASON YOU WERE LET GO?

As we've noted, people lose their jobs for a number of different reasons, and performance usually isn't one of them. Many of our clients tell us that the ostensible reason they were fired was performance-related— they were told they weren't a team player, sufficiently strategic, lacked cutting edge thinking, and so on—but the real reason was often as simple as their boss didn't like them. We discussed the generic reasons people are fired in a previous chapter; now, let's examine these reasons in greater detail.

- *The boss did it.* Perhaps you have a new boss who doesn't know you well and didn't hire you and wants to put in his own team. Perhaps a rift has developed between you and the boss over a difficult project. Perhaps your boss views you as a threat to his job. Whatever the reason, bosses fire people for a wide variety of reasons that have little or nothing to do with performance.
- *Restructuring.* Obviously, you know if you're being let go because of an economic downsizing, but you may not believe this is the only reason or the main reason. Even if 15 percent of the workforce was downsized after a restructuring, acquisition, or merger, you still feel singled out for punishment. Why were you in the 15 percent and

not Tom or Mary? Most of the time, it's because you were vulnerable. In other words, you were in a group that was overstaffed. Or you were the last one hired, first one fired. Or you happened not to have forged alliances with the right people. Or you were simply a victim of the numbers. When you feel that the restructuring was aimed at getting rid of "old-timers" or high paid workers, then it's hard to rebound from the experience.

  • *Politics.* People sometimes are fired because they refused to play politics in a political culture. Other times, they play and lose; they align themselves with a boss who becomes persona non grata. It seems as if people would know if they were fired because of politics, but this isn't always true. Or rather, they beat themselves up for choosing the wrong side, saying to themselves, "I should have been smarter than that!" Political battles within organizations can become nasty, and the losers often feel like career losers. If you've been on the losing side in such a battle, you should recognize that it's politics, not personal.

  • *Personality conflicts.* You may have been fired because you didn't get along well with your boss, your boss's boss, direct reports, or colleagues. As companies flatten their structures and move toward team-based work groups, the ability to work well with a diverse group and achieve consensus becomes crucial. If you're the type who works best on his or her own or has a low tolerance for consensus, you may have found yourself crossing swords with people working in teams. Or, you're being asked to tolerate Joe who is 20 years younger than you and has a very different work style. Or you're required to work closely with people from another function—a function your group has been at odds with for many years. You should recognize that in most instances, there's nothing wrong with you. In pressure-packed situations, personality conflicts are inevitable, and it doesn't mean that you're unable to work well with others. We understand, though, that this is exactly how it feels when you're fired.

In addition, some of you may tell others that you "retired" since that's how your organization termed your exit. In reality, the company made you an offer you couldn't refuse—you retired because they wanted you to rather than because you were ready to stop working. In these instances, you need to level with yourself and recognize that you were fired. Today, the common euphemism for what happened is "forced retirement." A *Business Wire* article (December 13, 2006) noted that in a Sun Life Insurance survey, 22 percent of all retirees are forced into retirement a few years sooner than they had anticipated, and that downsizing, layoffs, illness, and injuries were the primary causes. The survey found that these premature retirements caused significant financial and health insurance difficulties for these individuals.

We've found that these forced retirements can plunge people into bad moods, not only because they have to struggle with financial and health insurance issues, but because they have difficulty accepting the truth of what happened. Organizations sometimes sugar-coat these terminations by providing generous severance packages and by giving the event a positive label. As a result, people don't respond honestly and appropriately. Instead, they drift into a premature and often unhappy retirement, telling themselves they should feel fortunate that they got to retire early with a nice financial package, but feeling unsettled and manipulated. As a result, they have difficulty pinpointing the cause of their mid-career doldrums. They don't realize that they resent being forced to stop working before they were ready and that they feel "used by the organization." Identifying and accepting these feelings for what they are is important if you want to get on with your life . . . and your career.

OPPORTUNITIES AND OPTIONS

When you don't know the real cause behind your boredom, burnout, retirement, or firing, you can't respond to it effectively. Your false belief about why something happened will prevent you from emerging from your career blues and discover what you really want to do for the next 10, 20, or 30 years. If you believe you're burned out because you can't handle workplace stress, you'll be closed to any job opportunities that come your way. If you're convinced that you're bored because any job is boring after you've mastered it, then you're not going to consider the alternative of switching careers.

On the other hand, if you can pinpoint the cause of your career malaise, then you have the knowledge necessary to capitalize on opportunities and explore options. When you're aware you retired because your work had no purpose, you can start focusing on jobs, careers, or volunteer positions that provide you with a sense of purpose. If you realize you were fired because your boss was a bad guy, you'll have the confidence to risk being fired again for the reward of a satisfying job.

Therefore, let's look at the ways you can use what you know about the cause to pursue a cure for the mid-career blahs.

5

Use the Cause to Find the Cure

At this point, you should have a sense of why you're bored or burned out, or why you're reacting in counterproductive ways to your firing or retirement. Some of you may have a single cause for your career doldrums; you determined that you were bored because you were stuck in a well-paying job that you were good at but were reluctant to leave because of the security and benefits. More likely, however, your doldrums have multiple causes: you're suffering from Things Used to Be Better (TUBB) syndrome, you're burned out from working in a series of high-stress positions, or you're discouraged because you tried to retire and have found that you miss the challenge or the opportunity to make a difference.

Whatever causes you've discovered will help you solve the dilemmas and difficulties of mid-career change. To facilitate this process, we're going to suggest some common cures for each of the bored, burned out, fired, and retired causes. We're also going to caution you about the mistakes people make trying to escape their mid-career doldrums—mistakes that may seem like the right solution at the time.

As we begin with cures for boredom, keep in mind that you're going to need to filter our advice through your particular situation. What works for someone else might not work for you. We've tried to focus on the most common cures in each of our four categories, but it's possible that you'll need to tailor them to fit your specific circumstances.

THE CURES FOR BOREDOM

Boredom is deadly, and when you're in the throes of a boring job, it often seems as if the only possible cure is to quit. That may well be an option worth considering, and we'll explore the best ways of leaving a job. At the same time, though, consider other alternatives. If you recall, we listed seven common causes of boredom in the previous chapter, and we probably could have listed at least five more. Similarly, numerous ways exist to escape this boredom and find exciting activities at mid-career. Here are four possible responses to boredom we'd like you to think about:

1. *Enhance the job.* Most people possess more control over their jobs than they realize; they have the chance to infuse their jobs with greater challenge, meaning, and fun. Take advantage of that chance and see if you can tweak or even reinvent the job. It sounds obvious, but many people fail to ask their bosses for a tougher and more interesting assignment. Others become locked into a job routine that they could break if they simply tried experimenting with the way they do things or set new work goals for themselves. We know people who have found ways to work faster, freeing up time to take on new and more fulfilling work assignments. You can provide yourself with greater intellectual challenge or opportunities to be creative, but that means forcing yourself to vary the job's boring routine.

Betty, for instance, sold services for a temporary placement firm. As part of her job, she was required to do cold calling—she was expected to make 10 cold calls daily. While Betty loved selling, she found cold calling boring and uncreative. As a result, she postponed making cold calls for as long as possible, waiting until the last moment to do them—or tried to get to them between meetings and appointments during her busy day. For this reason, they weighed on her continually and made her feel that her whole job was dull and frustrating when, in fact, it was just one aspect of her job. When it dawned on Betty that she could do the calls first thing in the morning and get them out of the way, it changed her feelings about work. She could segregate the boring part of her job from 8:30 A.M. to 9:30 A.M. Even better, Betty realized as she began making her calls earlier in the morning she was more likely to reach people before they started their busy days.

2. *Change jobs within the company or change companies.* If you feel there's a major disconnect between you and your job or that you've been unhappy in your position for a long time, then a major change may be necessary. If you like your company and its culture, the solution may be to transfer to a different position, function, or office. Too often, people assume that they're stuck in the job they have. In reality, bosses may see that you would be more valuable to the organization in a different position. In other instances, of course, the cure for your boredom may reside outside your company. Bored mid-career people often are victims of inertia; they know they should make a change but find the thought of looking for a new job so daunting that they can't muster the energy.

Force yourself to start talking to your network of friends and colleagues about opportunities in other organizations. Visit Internet web sites, look at the want ads and make an active, continuous effort to explore other possible jobs—both inside your company and outside. These activities can be energizing and help you feel more in control of your situation. By keeping an eye on the market, you'll have a better sense of how competitive your salary and skills are and whether there's an area where you could benefit from some additional training.

3. *Find more interesting activities outside of your job.* If you're bored because you lack intellectual challenge or enough to do, it's not always possible to solve the problem quickly within the context of the job. Your boss may not allow you to take on more challenging responsibilities. You may not be in a position to look for a new job. If you're bored and stuck, though, you may be able to find greater purpose and meaning outside of work. Take up a new hobby or go back to an old one. Take a language course. Learn to play golf or tennis. See more movies. Join a book club. Get more involved in your local community. Plan a trip. It's important to have things in your life you look forward to doing, especially if going to work isn't one of them.

Too often, people who are bored at work let that boredom permeate their lives. They're so enervated from the drudgery of the day that it's all they can do to get themselves home, eat dinner and plop in front of the television. Don't allow your professional boredom to be mirrored by personal boredom. If you make an effort to do something interesting in your off hours, you may well find that it leads to a new passion or sense of purpose; you may start out thinking that volunteering at the church near your home has nothing to do with your career, but you may discover that this work is more important to you than you thought and that you want to devote more time and effort to it.

4. *Change your attitude about your job.* After all, attitude is simply a state of mind and it is something over which you have complete control. While some jobs are excruciatingly boring—you are repeating tasks you could do in your sleep—we're assuming that you now recognize that the worst thing you can do is accept this boredom as a given. Consider the possibility that the mind-numbing routine of a job may have as much to do with your approach to it as the job itself. At least it's worth a try to come at your job from a fresh perspective. Try and find a challenge within your job; is there a task or responsibility that you don't find boring; if you focus on this task or responsibility, does it give you a sense of purpose?

Make a game of attitude adjustment. Set an ambitious objective for yourself that has nothing to do with your boss' objectives, and focus on achieving it. For instance, let's say you're an outplacement counselor and you find writing resumes a repetitive and mindless task. You decide, however, to set the goal of becoming the best resume writer in the world. This means you turn the task into an art rather than a craft. You throw out the rules of resume writing and use your skill and experience to create resumes you know will set a new standard for quality. You work hard and creatively on these resumes, and soon you're taking pride in the end result. In this way, you've taken at least some of the boredom out of the job.

THE CURES FOR BEING BURNED OUT

The causes for burnout are as varied as those for boredom, though the cures for the former may require more significant actions. Boredom can often be relieved by varying an existing job or adjusting a negative attitude. Burnout sometimes demands a more creative cure. When you're working yourself into the ground, are extremely anxious or are under enormous stress, you may need to do more than just talk to your boss about easing the pressure or finding a better way of coping. You may, in fact, need to see a therapist. From time to time, that's exactly what we recommend to our clients.

Here are five of the most effective solutions we've found for mid-career professionals who feel stressed out:

1. *Take a break from your job.* At mid-career, many of you have been working for 20 or 30 years straight. It may be that you need anything from a long weekend to a longer vacation to a leave of absence in order to relieve the pressure you're under. Consider taking a break and giving yourself a chance to recharge. Your organization may allow veteran employees to take unpaid leaves, which is terrific. We've found that people use this break in different ways to gain breathing space. Some just need some alone time to reflect. Others use the time to travel. Still others find a retreat in some beautiful part of the country and read, walk, and relax. Determine which of these or other tactics will best help you restore your energy and diminish that burned out feeling.

2. *Find some balance.* We are big advocates of having a life beyond work. Too often, we see people who lack interests and activities that aren't work-related. These are the same people who we'll talk about in a bit—the ones who don't know what to do with themselves when they retire. As important as work is, failing to strike a balance between professional and personal lives invites burnout. Achieving balance varies from person to person. You may be someone who needs to spend more of your free time reading. Or you may be the type of person who requires regular physical activity. Of course, many people find the needed balance by spending more time with family and friends.

If you're a perfectionist, recognize how vulnerable you are to burnout, especially as you become older. Earlier in your career— perhaps before you married and had children—you might have been able to get away with a single-minded devotion to work and making sure all the *t*s were crossed and the *i*s were dotted. When you're in mid-career, however, your life is fuller and too many conflicting priorities exist to micro-manage every detail of your job. Similarly, if you have an all-consuming job, you may find the demands onerous in a way you didn't find them when you were younger and more ambitious. If either of these conditions describe you, seek balance outside of work. While you will still feel the pressure when you're in the office, you'll have a way of relieving it outside of the office. We've found that people who have healthy, fulfilling personal lives tend to be able to handle this pressure without burning out.

3. *Establish boundaries.* In other words, draw a figurative line in the sand and tell yourself that you will not do work or even think about it during certain times of the day and in certain places. Traditionally, work was done between 9 and 5, five days a week, with breaks for coffee and lunch. You naturally had boundaries guarding yourself from work at all these other times. With the advent of instant messaging, Blackberries, cell phones and numerous other technologies, the natural boundaries have faded. The mindset that people should be available to work and should be thinking about work 24/7 in order to maintain a competitive edge has further dulled these dividing lines.

Therefore, it's probably more accurate to suggest that you redraw the boundaries. Refuse to check e-mails when you're on vacation; don't call into the office when you're at lunch; don't work when you arrive home in the evening; reserve at least one weekend day for non-work activities. We cannot overemphasize how important it is to maintain these boundaries. They will quickly serve as an anti-burnout remedy if you make a conscious effort to keep them in place. If you need motivation to do so, think of all the times in the past when your boss called you at home or you cut short a vacation because of an "office emergency." With hindsight, you probably know that it was not an emergency at all; that your boss really didn't have to call you at home, and you really didn't have to truncate your vacation. It was only at the time that some snafu seemed more important than it really was.

4. *Seek help.* Request advice and counsel from people in your network. Talk to your mentor, colleagues you trust, friends, and family members. If you have access to a coach or you have a good

relationship with someone in HR, discuss how you feel with them. Keeping all that stress and anxiety inside is guaranteed to make it worse. Verbalizing it doesn't guarantee that it will instantly disappear, but we've found that "getting it all out" is an apt phrase to describe burnout related conversations. You are finding an outlet for all that pressure that has been building up inside of you. Sometimes, people will make positive, actionable suggestions; they may suggest ways for you to deal more effectively with impossible deadlines or even offer to help take some of the work load off your shoulders.

It's possible that the source of your burnout is a difficult boss, and if that's the case, you may need a coach, a support group, or a religious mentor to advise you how to deal with this individual. A good coach can teach you coping skills that will help you "manage up" and decrease the negative impact this boss has. The coach can also teach you how to do a better job of prioritizing so that you're not working seven days a week under constant deadline pressure. In addition, a coach can help you protect yourself from the tremendous anxiety many mid-career people experience. Yes, downsizing is a legitimate concern and it's possible that you're vulnerable, but you need to put this anxiety in perspective and recognize the skills and strengths that make you marketable.

5. *Identify your condition.* In other words, acknowledge that you're feeling burned out. This may seem like superfluous advice, but we've found that a significant percentage of our clients are in denial about how work pressure is affecting them. They recognize that they're "not themselves," but they downplay the stress, telling themselves to "toughen up" and rationalizing that everyone is feeling this pressure. It's only later—when they're in therapy, or when they've quit or been fired—that they realize that they were suffering from burnout. Don't wait for these events to happen. If you're feeling burned out, acknowledge that fact.

CURE FOR BEING UNHAPPILY RETIRED

Certainly retirement is the right choice for some mid-career people. If you're happy being retired and find fulfillment in traditional retirement activities, terrific. What is always the wrong choice, however, is wishing you could do something else but adopting a fatalistic attitude: "It's too late to change."

If you are unhappily retired, here are the cures:

1. *Rejoin the workforce in a full-time or part-time or consulting position.* This is easier said than done. After all, you officially retired. You told all your friends and colleagues you had had it and were ready to take it easy. Maybe they gave you a retirement party. Though you may feel embarrassed to "unretire," it's better than feeling useless or unfulfilled. Swallow your pride and invite everyone to an unretirement party. Start looking for positions. Ideally, if you were prepared to live on retirement income, you can be selective in the offer you ultimately accept. If you're someone who failed to think through the implications of retirement, join the club. Accept that you didn't really understand what retirement would be like and move on. If you deceived yourself about why you were retiring—if you pretended you were tired of working when in reality you were tired of being treated poorly by your boss—then you simply have to find a better job or company to work for. If you underestimated your need to work, don't beat yourself up for being obsessive or neurotic about it. Perhaps you're someone for whom your career has been a calling, or you derived a great sense of purpose from what you did. You thought you would gain the same satisfaction from playing with your grandchildren and volunteering once a week, but it wasn't the same. Congratulate yourself on recognizing how important work is to you and find a job.

2. *Determine your motivation for returning to work.* This is a critical step because many people unretire to jobs that throw them into another variation of the BBRF cycle; they find a job, but it causes them to be bored, burned out, or results in their being fired. In many instances, the problem is that people unretire without considering what they really want out of a mid-career work experience. Ask yourself if you want to get a job because you miss the camaraderie of a workplace, or do you simply need to supplement your income? Or in your temporary retirement, did you discover some passion that you want to turn into a business or a job? Or do you possess a skill that you believe can be of great use for a particular organization? Being painfully honest with yourself as you answer these questions will help you make the right mid-career move. You won't take the first job that offers or make the mistake of seeking full-time work when you should find a part-time position (or vice versa).

3. *Pursue a meaningful retirement.* By meaningful, we mean doing more than mere activities. If you love shopping, great. If you like watching television, fine. But many mid-career professionals who led busy, satisfying work lives need even more to do when they stop working. Don't fall into the retirement trap of puttering around the house and avoiding the harder task of discovering what to do with the rest of your life. Make an effort to think about and explore what type of retirement lifestyle will make you truly happy. Perhaps you should volunteer. Perhaps you should become more involved in your community. Perhaps you should start your own business.

It may take you a while to figure out what your real goal is and how to achieve it. In the interim, don't sit there waiting for something to happen. Instead, force yourself to stay active, learning, and involved. Get in good physical condition—it's more difficult to pursue a meaningful activity if you feel lethargic or fatigue easily. Strengthen your computer skills—whatever you end up doing, you're probably going to need to know your way around the Internet and master other technological tasks. Sign up for a computer class if you can't learn these skills on your own. Spend some time in bookstores and libraries and online researching different hobbies, careers, volunteer activities, and so on. Attend events in your community—lectures, support groups—where you can network and learn.

Recognize that you're going to have to blaze your own trail. You may have a friend who is perfectly happy to retire and read all day. You may have another friend who is partnering with an adult child in a business. You may know someone else who has gone back to school full-time at age 60. Be aware that the other person's path may not suit you. You need to make it your responsibility to investigate possibilities and reflect on and talk about what makes sense for you.

For instance, Peter was a vice president of communications for a large corporation, and he took advantage of a retirement opportunity during a downsizing. He knew a number of people who had left the corporate sector and found great satisfaction doing not-for-profit work, and he decided to devote himself to volunteer work. This devotion lasted 6 months, and he was miserable. Though Peter liked the idea of doing good, he needed the results, focus, deadlines, and tangible and intangible rewards of a high-powered executive position. To his credit, Peter recognized that he had to return to the corporate world and eventually found a new, satisfying job. He tries to give back by mentoring younger people in his organization, but he also recognizes that he does not want to spend the next 20 or so years doing volunteer work.

CURES FOR BEING FIRED

As difficult as it is to get past being fired at mid-career, it can be done. We have worked with hundreds of people who were fired in their forties, fifties, and sixties and bounced back. They found new jobs, careers, and interests that were even more rewarding than the ones they had before. Consider, then, these cures for being fired:

1. *Use being fired as a catalyst for learning and growth.* When you're fired because your boss had it in for you or because you had bad chemistry with the wrong person, the process is personal, not business. Some people respond to this personal attack on who they are by becoming a victim; they complain about the unfairness of it all and become mired in bitterness. Other people believe they had it coming. They feel they lacked the talent or knowledge necessary to do a good job and deserved to be fired, and their self-esteem is so low they're afraid to try anything else.

Don't fall into either of these doldrum-inducing traps. Instead, reflect on what it tells you about yourself. Have you reached the point in your life where you no longer are willing to tolerate incompetents? Do you want to avoid ever being placed in a situation like this again? With hindsight, is there anything you might have done differently to avoid the outcome of being fired? It's tremendously useful to learn if you have problems with certain types of people or bosses in general. While being fired is no fun, it can provide you with insights about situations and people that cause you problems. Next time, you should be better able to avoid these problems by being aware of what gets you in trouble. It may be that you should look for a job where your boss is the same age or older than you, you should stop working for others and start working for yourself, or you should make a greater effort to get along with people who have different work styles than you do.

2. *Use being fired as a way to evaluate the cultures and types of organizations where you want to work.* As common as restructuring and political infighting are in organizations today, you should assess whether this type of environment suits you, especially after losing a job because of it. Though being fired because your company had to downsize or because your group was aligned with the wrong executive is less personally devastating than because of alleged poor performance, it can help you rethink the type of work environment that suits you. Some mid-career people talk to us about being fed up with highly political cultures and unstable companies. They want to find a job where they don't have to play so many games or be worried about losing their job for economic reasons every day. Some people opt for smaller companies with more stable cultures, and are willing to trade off a certain amount of income for stability. Others accept the possibility of a downsizing but want to find more family-oriented cultures—they want to work for a company that values its people.

3. *Learn to turn it.* Recognize that being fired at mid-career can be a wake-up call. Many mid-career professionals need to be shaken up to be pushed to consider other possibilities. In social work circles there is an expression: "turn it." Social workers use it to refer to a negative situation that they want people to turn and look at from a fresh perspective. Being fired forces mid-career professionals to turn it— to look at their job situations and careers in a new way. After being fired, you're likely to view not only your career but yourself from a different angle. Sometimes this shift in perspective is all that's needed to glimpse opportunities that you previously missed. In addition, the

simple fact that you were fired often results in other people stepping up and offering you ideas and opportunities. When people learn you've been fired, they suggest job and career directions they probably never would have mentioned before. When you're fired, you may go through outplacement and be steered toward a better, more fulfilling job. And when you're fired, you may have both the time and the inclination to try something new. Being fired is no fun, but in its wake you may find a new job, career or workstyle that would not have been possible if you hadn't lost your job. We have seen this happen again and again. So often we hear: "Being fired was the best thing that could have happened to me."

RE-CAREERING: HOW TO MAKE A FRESH START

To implement any of the cures just described, you may need to accept that your old career is finished and your new one is about to begin. If you accept the possibility of a second, third, or fourth career, then you open your mind to other options besides the career track you've always been on. We are using "careers" in the broadest possible sense, since for some of you it may mean going back to school, getting a degree, and starting over in a completely different field. For others, it may involve finding a mixture of part-time and volunteer work. Whatever it is, recognize that re-careering is not just a possibility, but a trend. Not only are all types of organizations accepting of people who start late, but more opportunities exist for people in their forties, fifties, and older to find a calling. From volunteer jobs for seniors to Peace Corp positions for older individuals to virtual businesses where no one knows or cares about your age, openings exist for people who are willing to explore them.

We're not suggesting that re-careering happens overnight. For some of you, it might take years of education and training. As a society, though, we now accept and encourage multiple or episodic careers, so you should take advantage of this new norm.

The question is how. One of the biggest stumbling blocks for mid-career people is how to figure out what their next career should be.

Not everyone has harbored a specific dream of being a deep sea fishing boat guide or traveling to and working in a foreign country. With all the options that exist, it's easy to be confused.

To start eliminating this confusion, we have a simple exercise that we've found to be quite effective in giving our clients a general sense of what their next careers should be. Below you'll find a Preferences Scale, designed to help you identify what you value now. Concentrate on ranking each factor based on your feelings now, as opposed to how you may have felt in the past (what you valued 10 years ago you may not value as much now). For each of the values listed below, rank them from 1 through 5 based on how important each is to you:

5—very important

4—important

3—somewhat important

2—marginally important

1—unimportant

Financial success _____

Power _____

Autonomy _____

Security _____

Working under pressure _____

Stability _____

Working alone _____

Competitive peers _____

Influence _____

Fast pace _____

Collaboration _____

Creativity _____

Public contact _____

Managing _____

Change and variety _____

Decision-making _____

Recognition _____

Advancement _____

Challenging problems _____

Status/Prestige _____

Innovation _____

Risks _____

Friendship _____

Location _____

Structure _____

Altruism _____

Health _____

Family _____

Satisfying work _____

When you've completed this preference exercise, focus on the 4s and 5s. These should be the determining factors for whatever career or activities you decide to pursue. As you reflect on these factors, make an effort to consider how your work and life values have changed over the years. Do these changes suggest that your current activities or career are misaligned with your current values? What jobs or activities make sense given these values? What is feasible, both from a time and a financial perspective?

By thinking about these questions, you may be able to find an anti-doldrum path. It may not give you the specifics of that path, but at least it will start you in the right direction. To understand what that direction might entail, here are a few re-careering stories from our files.

CHALLENGING CHANGES: TWO PEOPLE WHO MADE THE SWITCH

Richard, a highly successful human resources executive for a top corporation, had over 200 employees reporting to him and a high-level executive role that allowed him to take on strategic and planning responsibilities. Despite a great salary and other perks, Richard was bored. There was clear disconnect between Richard and his job, a disconnect that had emerged in recent years and had become more pronounced. At first, Richard tried to fight through his boredom, telling himself that he had a cushy job that everyone envied. Finally, his wife pointed out to Richard (in response to Richard's complaints that he wasn't getting the same "charge" from work that he used to) that he might consider other career options besides just finding a new job. They talked about it, and Richard admitted that in the last few years, he had spent more than a few bored moments at work dreaming about starting his own business. Richard completed the Preferences exercise, and it clearly showed that what he valued in work had changed from earlier in his career— autonomy, creativity and challenging problems all received 5s, and 20 years earlier they received 2s and 3s. As a result of this knowledge, Richard began planning his exit from his corporation and started putting the pieces in place to start his own human resources consulting firm. He now has a solid business, and his former employer is his number one client.

Diana made an even more monumental re-careering move. A noted financial analyst working for a prominent investment firm, Diana's first few years were a grind. Over time, however, she demonstrated her skills and received a number of raises and commensurate salary increases. At 47, Diana was doing quite well, but after her last promotion she was placed in a high-stress position that involved tight deadlines, a significant amount of travel, and extremely challenging assignments. She was tired and often irritable, and she believed her job was taking a toll on her personal life—she was twice divorced and found she couldn't spend as much time as she wanted with her teenage daughter. She was frazzled, and fortunately, she recognized that it was work that was making her this way. She decided to take a sabbatical— her company agreed to give her three months off without pay. As Diana was enjoying what she called her "time out," she met a photographer's agent at a party who mentioned that a top fashion photographer she represented was looking for a studio manager. In college, Diana had taken photography and art classes, and had considered a career in that area before opting for an MBA and the more lucrative career it promised. Still, when the agent told her about the position, she decided to call the photographer and tell her she was interested. They met, hit it off, and agreed to give it a try. Diana found that even though this job had its own stresses and did not pay as much as her previous position, it did not produce the burned out feeling of her previous analyst job. Diana's life became sane again and, most importantly, she became reconnected with her daughter.

Diana's and Richard's stories are not anomalies. Instead, they are just two examples of the re-careering trend among baby boomer professionals and even older people. We could tell you hundreds of stories that have the same moral: Figure out why you're in mid-career crisis, determine your options to get out of it and then test the waters; you may discover a much more satisfying career than the one you're leaving behind.

6

Open Yourself to the New World of Work and Emerging Opportunities

As you consider the previous chapter's cures for the mid-career blues, we also hope you'll recognize all the opportunities that exist for people in their forties, fifties, or sixties who want to reinvent their careers or transform their lives. These opportunities more than offset downsizing and other troubling trends, providing mid-career professionals with greater flexibility if they want to continue in their current field and greater options for exploring new careers or ways of working. We have seen individuals who have used great energy and creativity to explore these opportunities, discovering interests and finding jobs that far surpassed their earlier careers—careers that they had always assumed they would have for life.

Are you aware of the opportunities that are both various and plentiful? Perhaps not. In fact, we've had more than one client enter our offices and say something to the effect that, "There's nothing out there for someone my age," or "with my background."

The reality is that there's plenty out there, but that a variety of factors conspire to make it seem like few opportunities exist. We want to shatter this misconception, and we're going to do so first by telling you a terrific story and then detailing a list of opportunities, and why they may not be obvious to you at first glance.

DESIGNING A NEW CAREER

Annie, 51, had a senior merchandising position in a women's apparel company and was responsible for sourcing the fabrics used in product manufacturing, working with marketing on pricing new designs, and controlling inventory. The sourcing part of her job was what she liked best, as it entailed traveling to Italy, choosing fabrics, and negotiating the prices with the manufacturers. She knew all the manufacturers well and enjoyed the camaraderie she felt with them. Over time, however, the long hours and high stress got to Annie, and she started feeling tired and unmotivated.

She lost her job when a new boss was hired from the outside and wanted to put his own team in place. Shortly thereafter, Annie decided she wanted to do something different, but related to the fabric area—she had a passion for fabric colors, design, and texture. She also had a good eye and thought she would be valuable to an interior design company or a fabric manufacturer.

Unfortunately, Annie found this field hard to break into—many of the companies were small and couldn't afford to pay Annie's salary. It was also a difficult time in the job market—it was one year after 9/11, the economy was on the downturn, and all companies were pulling back on hiring.

After 6 months of having no success trying to break into the fabric business, she accepted a job at a privately held small manufacturing company owned and led by a successful entrepreneur. She heard before she went to work that "the place was crazy." She didn't know how crazy. Everyone was at the whim of the owner, and little structure existed. Annie's organized approach was not valued. After 6 months, Annie and the company mutually agreed that things weren't working out.

Annie began working on two freelance projects as she pursued new employment opportunities. She had faith in her abilities, in her passion for her work, and her extensive network of contacts. If she persisted and was open to learning new things, she was certain she would find a great new job. Annie kept interviewing, but nothing happened. She wondered if her age or high salary requirements were turning off prospective employers.

Annie persisted until she had an epiphany. She recognized that she was looking in the wrong place for her opportunities, that top merchandising jobs with major retailers were few and far between, and smaller companies figured she was overqualified. Convinced from her solid freelance assignments that there was a place for her skills and experience, she decided to put what she wanted on paper. She started by creating the following list of what she loved most in her work:

- Meeting new people, building relationships
- Working with the designers and manufacturers on fabrics and colors
- Exploring ways to use new fabrics
- Colors, textures—mixing/matching, putting them together
- Negotiating, pricing, managing budgets

She began to think about how much she enjoyed decorating her New York apartment and how everyone loved it when they walked in the door. She also thought about all the friends she had assisted with their apartments. The idea of helping people decorate their homes struck her as what she wanted to do. She knew she couldn't do it in New York City—the competition was too great and the field was already overcrowded.

But what about near her hometown in Massachusetts—a commuter's community where people had enough money to be able to hire someone to help them decorate the interiors of their homes? It would also solve a major financial problem. There was no way she could start a business and afford to stay in New York. This was the hardest part of her decision. She loved the vibrancy of the city, but she was single and career oriented—being happy in her job was the most important thing to her. She wanted to be passionate about her work, and she realized that something had to give.

She investigated design courses she could take in Boston, which was commuting distance from her hometown. She contacted the Small Business Administration's Women's Business Development office to learn where she could take training in starting a business. She hired a financial planner to help her assess her financial situation and what it would take financially for this idea to work. She spent considerable time building a business plan—scoping out competition in the area, learning more about the client base, determining how she would get customers. This included everything from contacting old high school friends to joining local community organizations. She was optimistic about her sales ability. After spending 2 years looking for a job, she was fearless when it came to calling people and asking for meetings. Finally, she received a small loan for the startup costs of her new business, including marketing materials and administrative assistance, and that's when she made the move to Massachusetts.

Once there, she became involved in the community by volunteering to help redecorate the family center of a church she joined. Within a month, Annie received a job from a church member who was impressed by her worked and wanted Annie to help redecorate her living room. Over the next few months, the assignments began to trickle in, and soon the trickle became a healthy stream and Annie found that she had a growing business. With hindsight, she recognizes that she was burned out on the retail business and that her real opportunity was initially hidden from view. It took persistence and drive for Annie to figure out what the opportunity was, but when she discovered it, she realized that this was the work that she was meant to do.

As you'll discover, Annie's story isn't unique. Opportunities abound for mid-career professionals, but you'll need to open your eyes and your mind to discover them.

SIX INCREDIBLE OPPORTUNITIES

The glass is either half full or half empty. For example, when we tell clients about how they are in a perfect position to open a consulting business, they may respond one of two ways:

- "No way, consulting is what people do when they can't get a job."
- "You're right; I have the contacts and the experience, and there's a growing market of companies who are turning to small, independent consultants for help."

The latter attitude helps people materialize opportunities, while the former attitude hides them. We'll address this issue of hidden opportunities shortly, but first we want to give you a list of the most common opportunities that exist for mid-career professionals. We described some of these opportunities earlier, but here we want to focus on why they're so prevalent today, factors to consider before pursuing them, and what you can do to capitalize on them.

Part-Time Positions

We're seeing more and more part-time options available for mid-career people for numerous reasons. The job-sharing trend is one cause, but part-time positions also give organizations more economical options to get work done. As a result of outsourcing and internal cut-backs, they may prefer to have at least some people in a given work unit engaged on a part-time basis. Depending on the position, these companies may not have to provide office space or benefits for a given individual. We've also observed that retailers are looking for greater age diversity among their staffs in order to be more responsive to their increasingly aging customer base, and are willing to take on part-time people to achieve it. If you go into establishments such as Barnes & Noble and Crate and Barrel, you're likely to find part-timers who are in their fifties who relish reading and home decorating.

To understand whether you're interested in pursuing part-time opportunities, be aware that part-time means different things to different people. It can involve shorter hours—working 1 or 2 days per week, half days five days per week, or weekends only. It can also mean seasonal schedules—in the summer or during holidays. It can also entail special events or project work—an election campaign, helping plan an annual corporate event, and so on.

If you're in a good financial position, if you just want to keep your hand in, or if you want to get a sense of what a new field is like without making a total commitment, part-time positions are great. You may find a part-time job that requires the highly specialized skills you've honed over the last 20 or 30 years, or you may find something that requires skills most people possess. You might discover a permanent part-time job—one that involves a formal agreement with a company to employ you for a certain amount of hours or for specific projects—or one that is temporary and uncertain in terms of hours and duration. You should also be aware that some of our clients have kept full-time positions and taken on part-time jobs on the side, sometimes for additional income but mostly because they were interested in exploring another type of work.

One other benefit of some part-time positions is that they often offer benefits. As we noted earlier, this isn't always the case, but in most states, if you work 1000 hours for an organization they must offer you benefits.

On the negative side, part-time work isn't always easy to come by, especially if you're picky about what you will do, and a job search can be just as difficult as if you were looking for a full-time job. In addition, many people choose part-time work after being bored or stressed out, only to discover that a part-time job can be just as boring or stressful. Finally, remember that organizations have part-time work for a reason. It may be that your local hospital offers wonderful jobs for part-timers, but most of them require you to work a midnight shift. An organization may tell you that you only have to put in 20 hours a week, but you discover that to meet their objectives, you're working 40 hours. Nonetheless, if you've thought through why you want part-time work and how it fits with your mid-career goals, you're likely to find something that is viable.

How to capitalize:
- Identify your area of interest and test the waters. Apply for jobs that seem tailored to a field or subject that excites you.
- Figure out what part-time schedule will meet your specific requirements in terms of hours per week, flexibility, location, etc.
- Be willing to change part-time positions if one isn't working for you. Recognize that many part-time jobs are out there and that if one isn't right, another one might be.

Educational Retraining

People go back to school for three reasons: to learn for the sake of learning, to obtain a credential or certification, or to learn a new skill or trade. Any of these options can help mid-career professionals escape the doldrums, depending on their situations. Some people just need the intellectual stimulation a class in art, music, or literature can provide to compliment whatever they do for their careers.

Many schools are now offering older adults a wide variety of educational programs. Columbia University, for instance, allows adults to audit courses taught by the school's professors. Though they are asked not to participate in discussions, these auditing students are able to attend the courses that full-time students take. Google "lifelong learning" and you'll see hundreds of colleges and universities that offer the same kinds of programs.

Other mid-career people are more interested in obtaining degrees in areas where they hope to pursue second careers. We've known business people who have obtained degrees in education, law, environmental science, and a wide range of other disciplines. Fortunately, more and more schools are accommodating older students, providing alternatives for those who work during the day but can only take classes at night or on weekends. If you're interested in this possibility, though, make sure that you're passionate about whatever degree you're pursuing. The application process alone is a lot of work, and a full load of courses, with all the homework that implies, is not for the faint of heart. If you're uncertain, it may be better to start with an extension course to see how it goes before making this commitment.

Perhaps one of the biggest "boom" areas in education involves certification and licensing programs. While the requirements vary from field to field, these programs have proliferated in response to a growing demand. Real estate licensing courses, for instance, have popped up in just about every part of the country. Certified financial planning courses have also become more common, though these require more time and testing than real estate certifications. You can also gain certification or licensing in many other areas, from being a travel agent to running crafts-related workshops (i.e., scrapbooking).

Finally, many mid-career professionals are enrolling in skills training workshops, seminars and individualized instruction. A mind-boggling range of alternatives exist. For instance, the Foundation

Center offers training in managing nonprofits and in fundraising. What has really changed in recent years, however, are the number of courses offered online. Google "online education" and you'll be amazed at all the opportunities you'll discover.

How to capitalize:
- Determine whether you have the time, financial wherewithal, and interest to go back to school full-time. Be aware that educational shortcuts exist for certain career goals—you can gain certification as a life coach, a bed and breakfast manager, and a mechanic through short-term, intensive courses.
- Consider an apprenticeship option. We know of people who have aspired to be chefs, retailers, and even practitioners of alternative medicine, and used apprenticeships to gain the knowledge they need.

Volunteer Work

We have become a nation of volunteers, and anyone interested in donating their time for a good cause will find many opportunities. Whether you're interested in helping clean up the environment, working in a soup kitchen, or helping raise funds to fight a disease, you're likely to discover an opportunity no matter where you live. We live in a time when people, especially baby boomers, feel compelled to give back. Wealthy donors have set up foundations to fund volunteer efforts, and former Presidents Bill Clinton and Jimmy Carter have given volunteerism a high profile. In addition, web sites have proliferated that greatly facilitate the process of finding a volunteer position that's right for an individual. For instance, www.VolunteerMatch.org helps people discover the cause and specific tasks that they're passionate about, linking individuals who use the site to groups that need help.

As great as volunteering is for people with an altruistic bent, it can also be frustrating if you're not realistic about what this experience will be like. We've known a number of mid-career professionals who entered into these activities with great enthusiasm that lasted for two or three weeks. Because they had unrealistic expectations—they thought they were going to be on the front lines of a cause, engaged in vital, challenging work—they became as bored as they had been in their day jobs. Sometimes they were assigned tasks that seemed trivial and beneath them. Sometimes they resented the many hours they were putting in for no pay. Therefore, before volunteering, make sure you know what you're getting yourself into and that you're driven to do it.

How to capitalize:
- Understand what you want to get out of the volunteer experience. Do you want to make it your calling and pursue it full-time, or are you just interested in gaining some knowledge about what it's like to volunteer?
- Use your understanding to determine how much time you want to devote to volunteering and what you're willing to do. Are you willing to do clerical and other low-skill work, or do you want to use the knowledge and connections you've obtained over the years to do high-skill work?

Starting Your Own Business

Many people have started their own businesses after working for others, but today mid-career professionals are in better positions to do so than ever before. Many mid-career people are leaving organizations with sizable severance and retirement packages, sometimes in the six figures. Second, they're leaving with great expertise that translates well into start-ups of all different types. Third, the environment is right for the shift from working for others to working for yourself. As we've mentioned, many tasks formerly done within large organizations are being farmed out to smaller, outside groups. Fourth, the Internet makes it much easier to do the research and networking critical to getting a start-up off the ground.

But probably the most important reason that opportunities abound for mid-career professionals is that a significant percentage of you possess the energy and vision to start your own business.

We've counseled a large number of professionals who have had it with the corporate world, who are bored or burned out by down-sized organizations and insensitive cultures, and who have been fired from these companies or retired in disgust. They were driven to succeed on their own, and aggressively investigated how the knowledge, contacts, and skills they acquired over the past 20 or 30 years translated to a start-up business. In short, they made their own opportunities.

How to capitalize:
- Prepare a business plan (see Appendix 3). This seems obvious, but too many mid-career professionals we've talked to relate stories of trying to open a business on a wing and a prayer. Either they were naïve, overconfident, or both. While many former corporate executives bring great skills and resources to entrepreneurial ventures, they sometimes don't realize what running a small business entails; that it's not like running a division or department within a large organization. A business plan forces you to analyze strengths and weaknesses of a business idea as well as all the financial ins and outs.
- Be ready to market and manage your business. This is a big change for many executives who have done one or the other but not both. When you run a small business, one second you're selling, the next you're trying to hire a temp. Being good at and comfortable with both skills is necessary. This may mean taking a course in advertising or public relations, or it may mean meeting with a small business owner and getting some tips about how to manage a business effectively.
- Do your research. More specifically, do more than one kind of research. We've seen too many people start their own businesses based on the certainty that they've got a million dollar idea. To validate that idea, they ask their friends and family what they think, and of course, no one wants to crush their enthusiasm. When we say do your research, we mean three things. First, go on the Internet and use a search engine to determine who your prospective competitors are. You may discover you have a market to yourself, which is terrific. You may also discover that you have three serious competitors, which

means you may have to reconceptualize your product or service to differentiate it. Second, ask some people who will level with you what they think of your idea; make sure they know you want the unvarnished truth. Third, go directly to your market and ask them for their candid assessment of your product or service. If you've designed a new basketball shoe, for instance, go to a local athletic shoe store and ask people there what they think of it. If you can hire a market research firm, great, but these are three things anyone can do on their own.

• Decide if you're up for the risk. To capitalize on opportunities, you have to take some financial risk. While it's possible you might be able to interest others in backing you or obtain venture capital money, most mid-career professionals we know end up getting bank loans or using their own money. That's fine, but you need to feel that you can live with the risk. Otherwise, you're likely to fold your tent at the first sign of problems and never give your business a chance to succeed. Please don't misunderstand this point; we don't want to discourage anyone from opening up a business. In fact, we are more dismayed by how many great business ideas never saw the light of day rather than by how many people have started their own businesses and failed. The former group is huge and the latter group is relatively small. Still, you should think about the risks involved and whether you're ready to accept them.

Consulting

Some of our clients turn to consulting in between jobs, while others see it as a fresh direction for their careers. Consulting is something just about everyone who is bored, burned out, fired, or retired considers, since everyone knows a former colleague who became a successful consultant or has contacts with consultants they used when they were part of an organization. The volatility and uncertainty that dominates the business environment has made consulting a booming industry. On top of that, we've seen consulting expand from the traditional management consulting segment into all sorts of sub-specialties — information technology consulting, human resources consulting, benefits consulting, and so on. This means that anyone with a specific area of organizational expertise has the chance to translate this expertise into consulting. Consulting is great for certain professionals, especially those who relish the flexibility and independence. Being able to set your own hours, travel, and combine consulting with other activities (volunteering, being with family, etc.) is appealing to many people.

Jan Smith is a great example of an executive who saw a consulting opportunity and decided to take advantage of it. A vice president of a packaged goods company, Jan headed a marketing support function and possessed a wide range of skills: team-building, writing and editing, project management, event management, and so on. When Jan retired, she decided to become a consultant, and to that end sent a letter to prospective clients and referral sources that read like a laundry list of communications, marketing and management skills. No one responded with any business.

Jan gradually realized that she had to specialize in one area—an area where her talents dovetailed with a market need. After receiving feedback from others, Jan decided that her event planning expertise was her most marketable skill set, especially her ability to orchestrate events to catalyze change; she had been very successful at her previous employer at using employee town hall meetings to inform and educate employees about new marketing initiatives. Relying on direct mail and networking to spread the word about her specialized consulting business, she quickly received a few assignments. In the beginning, they didn't pay well, but Jan knew that she could use every project to demonstrate to future clients her ability to consult effectively on event-related assignments. Within a year, Jan's consulting efforts were an unqualified success.

How to capitalize:
• Plan beyond the first few assignments. Many individuals tell us that once they put up their consulting shingle, they quickly received one or two great assignments, but after that, nothing happened. They discovered that unless they had the desire and ability to market their services, it was tough to make a go of it. Therefore, if

you're going to consult, consider whether you have the capability to get more than one or two assignments, and if you're willing to do the marketing necessary to keep your consulting business thriving.

• Identify what you have to offer. Some people think that consulting is going to be a breeze because they worked as high-powered executives with well-known companies for years, and they built up a great network of people "who owe them." They find, however, that despite all this, they need to be very clear about what it is they bring to the table and how it will benefit a prospective client; this is something they may never have had to do when working for an organization, and they can't take advantage of consulting opportunities unless they learn how to do it.

Teaching

Good teachers are in great demand, especially those with real world experience. Earlier we noted that many colleges were offering adult education courses, and these courses require teachers. Similarly, private and charter schools are increasing in number, and they too are looking for instructors. Unlike public schools, they usually don't require strenuous academic certification. On top of that, some large corporations have created their own in-house universities and require teachers with expertise from all organizational functions. Fourth, in an economic move, more business schools are adding adjunct professors to supplement their full-time professors. Typically, adjuncts are either working executives or have spent many years in a managerial capacity.

We know that the last thing some of you want to do is teach a subject that you've lost interest in. You may have spent 35 years as a marketing executive and you have no interest talking to others about marketing. You should also be aware that not everyone makes a good teacher. Just because you know a subject well doesn't mean that you can do a good job of communicating it to neophytes.

Teaching possibilities, though, run the gamut. We've known executives who have gone back to school, received their certificate in education, ended up teaching kindergarten, and loved it. Others have decided they want to teach a hobby they've become expert at—pottery-making or automobile repair. And there are those who just want to share their knowledge with others on a part-time basis—they become guest lecturers or teach special courses offered only in the summer.

How to capitalize:
- Translate your work experience into teaching assignments. Use your impressive resume as the cornerstone of a proposal to a local college or university. Be very specific in your proposal as to the type of course you want to teach, your credentials for teaching it, and how students will benefit from the course.
- Evaluate all the teaching possibilities. Don't limit yourself to one university and give up if a job falls through. Consider teaching as part of a corporate university or training program, think about giving workshops or seminars (either on your own or as part of an existing entity), explore teaching abroad, and expand your definition of teaching to include everything from hobbies (i.e., teaching framemaking at a local art supply store) to charitable efforts (tutoring kids from low-income neighborhoods). Certification is available for teaching English as a second language.

Given the six areas of opportunity discussed here, you would think that few mid-career people would be in the doldrums with all the exciting options available to them. The problem, of course, is perception. Let's look at why otherwise smart and savvy mid-career professionals are oblivious to all the opportunities that exist.

FIVE BARRIERS THAT OPPORTUNITIES HIDE BEHIND

We know that some of you are skeptical about the hopeful trends and events that we just summarized. This is perfectly understandable, since after being mired in the BBRF syndrome, you may not feel like things could possibly go well again. We want to reassure you that not only can things go well but that you are in an excellent position to make them go well. The key, though, is not allowing one negative event or mood to prevent you from taking action.

To avoid this, we'd like to explain why things sometimes appear worse than they are to mid-career professionals. Consider the following five barriers to perceiving opportunities and the optimistic realities behind them:

1. *The Daily Grind.* People become so caught up in the demands of their jobs, family crises, and a million other distracting elements that they miss what's really happening all around them. They lack the time, energy, and perspective to reflect on second career possibilities or volunteer positions. Ask them what they would do if they could do anything they wanted and they'll reply, "Who has time to think about things like that." As a result, the notion of finding a teaching position or starting their own business appear as remote as some distant planet. They don't put two and two together and recognize that these opportunities are plentiful and that they have the resources to capitalize on them.

We recommend that mid-career professionals force themselves to take a "time out" from the daily grind and reflect on the events and trends taking place outside of their work routines or personal problems and responsibilities. In other words, do some reading about work trends. Talk to other mid-career professionals about what they've observed and done, especially those who have left boring jobs or rebounded well after being fired. By doing this type of thing, you can give yourself a better view of opportunities that might exist for you.

2. *Lack of Exposure.* If you've worked in a large organization for most of your life, you probably haven't been exposed to the world of entrepreneurship, volunteering, part-time jobs, and so on. Surprisingly, perhaps, organizational work can be a narrowing rather than a broadening experience. You rarely meet professionals from the not-for-profit sector or interact with small business people. Though you may do as we suggest to escape the daily grind, you can still miss opportunities because you lack contact with individuals in other areas.

The solution, therefore, is to get that exposure. Volunteer once on the weekend at a local church or other group. Through your network, arrange to have lunch with someone who has spent his or her life working in the not-for-profit world. If you know someone who runs a small company, visit that person's place of business. These interactions may give you a truer sense of what's possible for your career and your life.

3. *The Volatility of the World.* We've talked about the fast-changing nature of work earlier, but here we want to suggest that the dizzying pace of change is intimidating to many people. Suffering from information overload, they tune out a lot of fresh information. Consequently, they miss developments that may be relevant to their careers. By filtering out information, they don't see how an event may open doors for them in another field or allow them to make a switch to the not-for-profit sector.

The key here is staying informed. Mid-career professionals owe it to themselves to read relevant publications, monitor web sites, and do everything possible to keep ahead of the curve. Yes, all the changes in their field and elsewhere may feel overwhelming, but the way to manage this feeling is to stay current.

4. *Lack of Confidence.* "I can't work in an art gallery; I'd have to go back to school and get an art history degree." Or, "Sure, it would be great to start my own restaurant, but restaurants fail all the time, and I've never been in that business." We hear these statements all the time, and while they may contain some truth, that's not the point. These self-doubting attitudes prevent people from looking into things and discovering opportunities. From the get-go, they don't give themselves a chance to see what's possible in a given area.

Though it's silly to go to the other extreme and be overconfident, we recommend a cautiously optimistic mindset. Give yourself the benefit of the doubt; tell yourself it's possible that you might be able to beat the odds and open a successful restaurant. In this way, when an opportunity comes along, you won't automatically dismiss it and can evaluate it objectively.

5. *Complacency.* In other words, you fail to see opportunities because you've resigned yourself to your mid-career doldrums. You tell yourself it could be worse. At least you have a job. Or at least you have your retirement benefits. Part of the problem is that you know other people in your situation who are complacent, and you lack good mid-career role models who have escaped their doldrums. The norm

is sticking out a boring job until retirement, or spending retirement in front of the television rather than doing something you're passionate about. Complacency makes it appear as if opportunities are like mirages in the desert—pure illusion.

The cure for complacency is to find a mid-career role model who has demonstrated that opportunities are not mirages. If you look around, you're bound to find an ex-executive who has turned his hobby into a successful business or a downsized manager who has found a much more rewarding job in another field. These role models shatter the myth that you need to settle. We've talked to a number of professionals in their fifties and sixties who feel like it's time to "slow down." Why? That's not the attitude of Carmel, our 86-year-old friend, who attends yoga classes five days a week, or Jerry, a 78-year-old author and lecturer, or Dana, a 65-year-old who participates in three marathons a year. Look at all the politicians who run for high office in their seventies. Refuse to fall for the slowing down argument and let it blind you to the opportunities that are out there.

USE YOUR ROLODEX, RESILIENCE, AND OTHER MID-CAREER RESOURCES

Contrary to what some people may believe, it is easier to capitalize on career opportunities when you have 20 or 30 years of work under your belt than when you're starting out. While novices may have the advantage of boundless energy and a willingness to work for peanuts, they lack your tangible and intangible resources. If you doubt this statement, try the following exercise:

Place a check mark next to the following tangible resources you believe you possess:
- ❑ Information contacts—people who can provide you with insights and information to help you with an opportunity
- ❑ New business contacts—people who can provide you business or referrals to business
- ❑ Support contacts—people who can provide you with business services that you can't provide on your own

- ❑ Marketable expertise
- ❑ Concrete skills and experience
- ❑ Money (or the ability to obtain it) that will facilitate going after an opportunity
- ❑ Equipment—i.e., computer, cell phone, and so forth that are necessary for you to pursue an opportunity
- ❑ Office space

Place a check mark next to the following intangible resources you believe you possess:

- ❑ A willingness to take reasonable risks
- ❑ A positive attitude
- ❑ A sense of humor
- ❑ The ability to rebound from setbacks
- ❑ Strong business instincts
- ❑ The ability to negotiate/get deals done
- ❑ Relationship-building skills
- ❑ Patience
- ❑ Self awareness (know both your strengths and weaknesses)
- ❑ Decision-making expertise
- ❑ Conflict resolution ability

Circle the checked tangible and intangible assets that you feel you can use in pursuit of your opportunity of choice.

The odds are that you've circled at least a few items on each list. As you'll discover, these resources are invaluable, giving you a significant edge over younger people who lack some or all of these resources.

Now we'd like to focus on three specific resources that we feel are especially important from an opportunity perspective and how best to cultivate them:

Contacts

Mid-career professionals make two common mistakes when it comes to opportunity-related networking: They either ask too much, too fast, or they ask too little, too late (or don't ask at all). We advocate a middle ground that we call the *soft approach* to networking. This means using the process to seek advice rather than requesting a specific thing—a job, business, other contacts from their Rolodex. Most people are put off by individuals who make a direct appeal for "big" things. On the other hand, most people are flattered when they're asked for help and are usually more than willing to offer something of value that can be used to capitalize on an opportunity.

Therefore, start out by listing all the people you know or with whom you've worked. At mid-career, you probably have accumulated a lot of people. Though this sizable number may make the task seem daunting, don't be put off or take short cuts. Develop as comprehensive a list as you can, keeping in mind that each person on the list can lead you to others; that one individual who may not seem to have much influence may connect you to someone with a lot of clout. Make a conscious effort to add to and update this list regularly. Prioritize the names on the list and set up information interview dates, starting with the high priority names.

Successful networking has a lot to do with consistent, organized effort. For instance, when you make a call to set up an appointment, you should review what you want to communicate prior to the call— who referred you, explaining what type of advice and information you're seeking, and so on. You should also keep detailed records of each meeting, since if you're an assiduous networker, you're going to have a lot of meetings and you want to keep track of what each person suggested, who referred you to whom, and so on.

We've included a 13-step networking process (see Appendix 2) to help facilitate your networking.

Before going on to another resource, we want to leave you with some sample conversational openings you can use to approach colleagues, suppliers, customers, and others for assistance. One of the most challenging aspects of networking is breaking the ice and requesting information or a meeting. Here are some openings you can adapt for your own purposes:

- "I recently retired from _____, and I'm now thinking of going into consulting and would love to tap into your experience and see if you think this would be a good fit for me."

- "You've been such a successful teacher, and since I'm now thinking about going into teaching, I'd like to spend a little time with you learning what you like and don't like about the field."
- "After a number of years working for a large organization, I now want to start a business. I'd value your insights about what you experienced when you started your business."

Attitude

We recognize that some of you may lack the energy or drive necessary to seize an opportunity, especially immediately after a negative career event takes place. You hear about an emerging industry with a lot of jobs, but you say to yourself, "Why make the effort; I probably won't be hired."

The answer to that question is: If you don't make the effort, you definitely won't be hired.

Fran made the effort, in large part because she had a great attitude. Fran, a 48-year-old lawyer, had worked in the legal department of a packaged goods company for a number of years and then moved to a law firm where she oversaw training of new lawyers. She liked her job, but she got caught up in a restructuring.

Fran decided to look for a job like her previous one, but while she looked, she also wanted to explore working for a nonprofit organization, as well as law school teaching possibilities. She had been active in the association for professionals who work in training and development for law firms, and decided that she would keep her membership active—even though it meant she now had to pay for it herself.

Over the next year and a half, she built a portfolio career. She got a job teaching a class at a law school, she began doing project work for the Legal Aid Society and she started working as a consultant for law firms and the local law school career office.

She interviewed for five full-time positions, came in as the number two candidate for three of them and decided the two others were not a good fit. She also interviewed for two nonprofit jobs, but in the end she and the organizations realized the jobs weren't big enough. Each rejection disappointed her, but she never let it get her down or deter her from moving forward. She kept building her skills and experience, trusting that this strategy would pay off. She focused on learning and keeping herself visible—appearing on panels, writing a piece for a law journal, agreeing to teach a second course at the law school, and becoming active in her daughter's school.

Though Fran wasn't making quite as much money as she did at the law firm, she was getting by and doing things she enjoyed. Then she received a call from a search firm that was recruiting for the head of development at a highly prestigious law firm. She decided to throw her hat in the ring and, after an extensive interview process, was hired four months later. It's turned out to be a great job. Fran has had to give up all of her other jobs, but will probably someday go back to teaching and is determined to get herself on a nonprofit board at some point in the future. We should also note that Fran was hired because her resume showed broad, diverse experience since leaving the original law firm. All of her experience—teaching, coaching, managing projects, even her school activities—was relevant to what she would be doing in her new job and put her ahead of the traditional candidates coming out of traditional jobs.

If you lack Fran's positive attitude, here's a technique we've used with clients that often prompts them to take positive action. We call it the "Downside Analyzer": List all the downsides to pursuing a given opportunity. Ask yourself what is the worst thing that can happen if you call a colleague for advice, take a class, volunteer, or investigate starting a business. List the worst possible outcomes in terms of time, money, and people. How much time is required to take a given action, how much money do you need to spend, and what is the worst possible thing someone can tell you in response to your action?

Most people find that the Downside Analyzer reveals there really isn't much to lose, and that there's a lot to gain. This technique really helps you consider your situation from a low-risk, high-reward perspective, and that perspective fosters a positive attitude.

Sense of Humor

This might seem like an odd trait in terms of seizing opportunities, but we've found that it's absolutely essential in order to take some risks and be sufficiently persistent when embarking on a new path. Humor allows you to laugh off rejection when you try and fail to obtain a new job. Humor also helps you put your quest in perspective. You're not trying to be the first mid-career professional to become an astronaut. Instead, you're simply trying to explore a new career area, to learn something new or to contribute to the community. When things don't go according to plan, you can make fun of yourself and move on. Humor will help you avoid being discouraged and keep you focused on goals that are highly achievable—if you persist.

DEGREE OF DIFFICULTY: RECOGNIZE THAT SOME TRANSITIONS ARE EASIER TO MAKE THAN OTHERS

Not all opportunities are alike. As optimistic as we are that mid-career professionals can embark successfully on new careers and ventures, we should add that some of you will face more challenges than others. For example, if you're a high-powered, well-connected executive, you may have a relatively low degree of difficulty as you transition into consulting. If, on the other hand, you're a high-powered, well-connected executive who decides to go back to school, obtain a teaching certificate and become a kindergarten teacher, you have set the opportunity bar higher.

We write this not to discourage you from attempting ambitious transitions but to make sure you're realistic about them. In this way, you won't be as likely to be thrown off your path when you encounter obstacles. Being aware of what you can expect as you make a transition can make it much easier to handle the challenges.

To this end, we'd like you to think about the degree of difficulty that accompanies your particular opportunity. Here are some questions to reflect upon as you move forward:

To take advantage of your opportunity, do you need to:
- ❏ Acquire a completely different skill set?
- ❏ Go back to school full-time to obtain a new degree?
- ❏ Transition to a significantly different working environment?
- ❏ Adjust to working for yourself rather than someone else (or vice versa)?
- ❏ Move from a large organization to a small one?
- ❏ Change your work behaviors (i.e. become a seller of your own services rather than a manager of others)?
- ❏ Go from being a highly-paid professional to a lower-paid one (or not being paid at all in a volunteer role)?
- ❏ Develop humility in order to make the transition (working for a boss 20 years younger than you; having to sell others rather than being the customer)?

Again, even if you made check marks next to all of these questions, you shouldn't shy away from the challenge if it's what you really want to do. As you've seen throughout this book, other mid-career people have achieved highly ambitious second career goals against steep odds. You can too, but only if you're realistic about what your particular opportunity requires of you.

7

Enter Your Discomfort Zone: Transitioning to a New Way of Working

As you pursue the opportunities we've just described, you may find yourself confused, questioning, and anxious. As you embark on a not-for-profit career after spending years in the for-profit sector, or when you start working part-time after being a full-time employee, you're likely to experience at least some disorientation. This is to be expected. In fact, it's a good sign. When you make any significant transition, be it in work or in life, you're bound to experience some degree of discomfort. This passage to a new and better way of working isn't always smooth, but feeling uncomfortable is a sure sign that you're making progress through this passage. If you don't feel any trepidation, you probably aren't moving in a significantly new and challenging career direction.

Our goal here is to help coach you through your discomfort. We've worked with all sorts of mid-career professionals going through all sorts of transitions, and we've found that when they become comfortable with the discomfort, it can facilitate the transition process. Once people come to terms with the fact that their new career or interests aren't the same as their old ones, they can adjust to their discomfort.

How do you become comfortable with the discomfort? The first step is being realistic about what a major career transition involves.

BE AWARE OF THE STAGES OF DISCOMFORT

Certainly you've gone through other work transitions earlier in your career—receiving a promotion, taking a new job, receiving an overseas transfer, and so on. The odds are that these transitions created some anxiety, but most of them probably were of the minor variety because you remained on familiar ground. You weren't trying to launch a new career or spend most of your time volunteering instead of going to a corporate office. Most mid-career transitions involve big changes.

As result, you're going into the unknown. Your old routine may have been boring or the cause of burnout, but it at least was relatively predictable. Now, your identity may be on the line. In your previous career, you had a label such as "executive," "teacher," and so on. You had familiar colleagues in the workplace who provided support, a steady and perhaps sizable paycheck, and a business card with your identity embossed on it. For a good portion of your career, you probably felt your work had purpose and you took pride in your proficiency at it.

When you're in the career doldrums and haven't yet embarked on a new path, you can cling to your old identity and take comfort in it. You can tell yourself that you're going to find another job just like the old one, or you can fool yourself into believing that you had a great career and now you're perfectly happy puttering around the house all day. Once you decide to make a transition, however, your discomfort kicks in.

In Elizabeth Kulber-Ross' classic book, *On Death and Dying*, she described the five emotional stages of the grieving process: denial, anger, bargaining, depression, and acceptance. We've found that the discomfort of mid-career people going through transitions mirrors these five stages. We don't want to make a facile analogy, recognizing that losing a loved one is a much different and more emotionally impactful experience than losing a job. Nonetheless, the five stages of grieving are useful because people often underestimate the emotional aspects of grieving the loss of a career. As a result, they get stuck in a stage and never make it through their transition successfully. We've found that just being aware of these five stages creates the awareness necessary to move on. Therefore, let's look at each stage in terms of careers:

• *Denial*. Professionals making major transitions often start out denying that they're feeling uncomfortable. They may tell others that "things are great," and they may tell themselves the same thing. In reality, they doubt their ability to make a transition successfully.

• *Anger.* As they struggle in their transition, they blame others for their problems. Former bosses are often good targets for their ire. Instead of acknowledging that the transition period is tough, they displace their feelings by getting mad at an individual or a larger entity—they rail at the changes in their field that are forcing them to change how and where they work or they obsess over colleagues or competitors they view as more successful.

• *Bargain.* In other words, they negotiate with themselves: "If I don't make a go of this new business in a year, I'm going back to my old job." Or, "If this volunteering doesn't make me happy, then I can always just play golf all day." Bargaining is a way of avoiding the fact that the transition makes them uneasy; they're giving themselves an out if it makes them too uneasy.

• *Depression.* During this transitional period, people experience both inappropriate lows and highs. They're devastated when a prospective customer for their new business doesn't return their calls, and they're ecstatic when calls are returned. Many times, their reactions are related to their lack of confidence. During a transition, it's difficult to know if you're doing the right things or doing them well. Unlike in a large organization, the traditional measures don't exist. Therefore, a little voice in the back of people's heads suggests that they're not going to cut it, and this creates a depressed mood.

• *Acceptance.* This is the light at the end of the tunnel. At some point, mid-career people come to terms with their feelings, having worked through the previous four stages. They accept that there's no going back, and that they're actually able to look forward to the next stage of their careers and lives.

The key to this emotional process is avoiding getting stuck. We've seen some mid-career professionals who hit a bump in the road as they're making their transitions, and instead of moving on, they are consumed with anger. All they want to do is complain about how poorly they've been treated and how unfair everything is.

We recognize that this is a perfectly natural reaction. It's unnatural and unproductive, though, to get mired in any of the first four stages. We've found that in this regard, a little awareness goes a long way. People often become mired in a stage of their career transition without even knowing it. Once they become aware of it, they can extricate themselves and move.

To that end, look at the following checklist of behaviors indicative of people stuck in each of the first four stages. Determine which ones apply to you:

Denial
- ❏ Paint a falsely rosy picture of your new business to former colleagues.
- ❏ Refuse to ask anyone for assistance, even though you need it.
- ❏ Reassure your family that your new venture is going to earn you more money than your old job, even though you have serious doubts that this is true.
- ❏ Avoid specifics when talking with others about your new career or other endeavors.

Anger
- ❏ Find yourself complaining about your old boss when things go wrong in your new career.
- ❏ Lose your temper frequently or out of proportion to the cause when you're at work.
- ❏ Blame other people when things don't go smoothly rather than accept responsibility.
- ❏ Find yourself waking up in the middle of the night furious at something that happened in your old job.

Bargain
- ❏ Tell yourself more than once that if something positive doesn't happen in your new pursuit, you're going to return to your old career.
- ❏ Make unfavorable comparisons between your old career and your new one.
- ❏ Make a lot of "if only" statements, such as, "If only this new job paid more, I'd be happy."

❑ Give yourself unreasonable deadlines for success/happiness, such as saying that if you don't land an account by the end of the month, you're going to do something different.

Depression

❑ Beat yourself up for not being smart enough or aggressive enough to make it in your new endeavor.

❑ Become wildly happy and unrealistically optimistic when something goes well and become deeply unhappy when even a small thing goes badly.

❑ Feel lethargic or lacking your usual energy as you try and make your new venture viable.

❑ Think you've let others down or failed to live up to your potential as you struggle with your transition.

If you have two or more check marks in any of the four stages, it suggests that you may be stuck. This is especially true if a given feeling or behavior persists. If you just feel kind of down and lacking energy after a difficult day volunteering, that's natural. If you feel this way a few times a week for over a month, that probably means you're stuck in the depression stage.

Finally, we also want to give you a checklist that indicates you've made it to the acceptance stage and that you're ready to pursue a second career or activity with diligence and commitment:

Acceptance

❑ Rarely if ever dwell on your past career and what you're missing in present career.

❑ Feel as if you're in the "flow" of things; that despite the obstacles you may face, you are in your element.

❑ Spend a lot of time doing whatever it is you want to do with this second stage of your life rather than asking questions about it or complaining.

❑ Relish climbing the learning curve of your new endeavor, even when you must learn from mistakes you make.

Most of our clients make it to this Acceptance stage sooner or later. A bit later in this chapter, we'll provide some advice designed to help you reach Acceptance sooner. First, though, we'd like to introduce you to Matt, who struggled and was stuck in his transition for a while, but found a way to move on.

SURVEYING A NEW LANDSCAPE

After a successful 25-year career doing institutional sales at a large brokerage firm, Matt began to suffer from both job boredom and burnout. The combination of doing the same tasks repeatedly and the increasingly burdensome policies his firm imposed took its toll on Matt. Fortunately, he and his wife, Bev, had a decent amount of money saved and he could act on his desire to turn his weekend gardening hobby into a new career. Matt resigned from the brokerage firm and apprenticed himself to a local landscaper he knew. Ultimately, Matt wanted to open his own landscape business, and this landscaper was in his late fifties and saw Matt as a potential successor or buyer of his business. Initially, Matt envisioned himself designing elaborate gardens and working outside, but he quickly realized that outdoor work was physically taxing and not exactly what he had had in mind for himself at age 50. He realized his financial acumen and business sense were valuable in the "back room" of the business, and so he spent more time there than outside.

This unexpected hitch in his plans made him anxious. Had he made a mistake? Hadn't he wanted to do outside work instead of be stuck in an office? He loved his weekend gardening, and wasn't that what he wanted to expand into full-time work? At first, Matt denied these doubts, convincing himself that this was a great opportunity to use his business savvy in an area he was passionate about. Then, he became angry at himself as he realized how little money he was earning and how he had left a perfectly good job. The very relaxed nature of the landscape business—at least compared to his former job—caused Matt a great deal of anxiety and he began making deals with himself; he decided he would stick it out for a few more weeks, and if he wasn't convinced this was right for him, he would go back to the brokerage business. A few weeks passed, and Matt went back and forth about whether he was doing the right thing. At one point, Matt reached the conclusion that he really didn't want to own a landscaping business and take on all the office work that came with it. Though this was a good thing to learn, it left Matt with one fewer option, and this caused him some sleepless nights and the admission to his wife that he was "a bit depressed."

What helped Matt snap out of his funk was both time and a heart-to-heart talk with the landscape business owner. In terms of the former, Matt needed a month or two to become accustomed to his new identity—he had to come to terms with the reality that he was no longer a business executive. During his talk with the owner of the landscaping business, he talked honestly about what he enjoyed in the job, but he also confessed some of his uncertainties. The owner told him that he had become a valuable member of his small company and he would do anything within reason to keep him there. This included a shot at some design work as well as more buying opportunities—trips to nurseries to help select plants, trees, and other elements for a client's design. Matt eventually accepted the reality of his new situation. He loved the creativity and activities in the landscaping business, but he didn't like the drudgery of the paperwork. However, it was a tradeoff he was willing to make. He eventually became a full-time employee and he no longer had any doubts that he had found the right job.

WIDEN YOUR COMFORT ZONE

To help our clients deal effectively with the discomfort of mid-career transitions and reach the Acceptance stage, we ask them to consider the idea of a comfort zone. A comfort zone is anything that feels normal. Anything that is outside your comfort zone—be it positive or negative—is going to at first be viewed negatively. For instance, the tasks that you've routinely performed as part of your job for months or years feel comfortable. If you're given a stretch assignment—if you're asked to manage your company's Hong Kong office and you've never lived or worked in Hong Kong—then you're going to experience some discomfort. Be aware that discomfort can result from positive as well as negative events. For instance, the assignment to head the Hong Kong office may be considered a big promotion. You may feel gratified that you received it, but you may feel uncomfortable about living and working in another country or meeting the ambitious goals of the assignment.

During transitions, many people fight against these feelings of discomfort or do everything possible to avoid them. Unfortunately, this reaction prevents learning and growth at mid-career. What you need to do instead is "go into the pain." That sounds worse than it actually is. In other words, we're suggesting that you accept a moderate degree of discomfort as a sign that you're on to something, that the anxiety or unease that you're experiencing indicates that you're learning something new. By staying with it rather than running from it, you are able to widen your discomfort zone.

To help you develop a tolerance for discomfort, we recommend the following:

- Probe the why behind the discomfort. Ask yourself the following questions:
  - Why am I feeling uncomfortable; what about the situation is causing me to feel uncertain, scared, or incompetent?
  - Is my discomfort so intense that I don't think I can continue in my new direction; or is the discomfort anxiety-producing but tolerable?
  - If I weren't going through a mid-career transition, would I be feeling this level of discomfort? Is my concern about my new career direction intensifying my feelings beyond what they should be?
  - What is my worst fear? If I'm feeling anxious because I don't seem to be shining in my new job, what is the worst possible outcome? Is this worst outcome really that terrible, and if it comes to pass, do I have other alternatives?

We would urge you not only to ask these questions of yourself but engage in dialogue with others relative to these issues. You'll discover that anyone who has ever made a major transition in his or her life will have a story to share about similarly uncomfortable feelings. It helps to realize that discomfort is natural and that it's a temporary feeling. It's perfectly normal to feel nervous and have self-esteem issues when you have to solicit business for the first time (after years of having others solicit business from you), for example.

• Let go of the past. You're feeling so uncomfortable in your new situation because you're clinging to your old one. You can take the edge off your discomfort by releasing the anger and regrets about whatever took place. We have had a number of clients who start out every meeting with us by saying something like, "If only I would have done x . . ." They are fixated on mistakes made and paths not taken. Other mid-career professionals have less specific complaints, but they're no less insidious. They talk about how they'll never make the kind of money they used to or how they miss being the center of attention.

When you dwell on the past in this manner, you become stuck in the denial or bargaining stages. You turn your back on the discomfort that comes with pursuing a new direction rather than embracing and widening it. The following exercise may help you deal better with the anxiety of a new career.

Create a list of all the things you miss about your old career. It can be anything from a plush corner office, to a team of direct reports, to perks like flying first class. Make the list as long as you want, type it on a computer program and print it out every morning for one week. Each morning, take the printed-out list, crumple it up, and throw it in the trashcan.

This is a good, symbolic way to remind yourself that what's past is past. When you stop clinging to it, you'll find that you'll stop making unfavorable comparisons between then and now. It's critical that you let go of the past in order to move forward.

• Give yourself permission to muddle around for a while. We actually talk to our clients about "the muddle phase." Not only is this okay, but it's required. Transitions are not straight lines, at least for most people. You may need to try three different things before one really clicks. You may find that your dream of starting your own business wasn't what you thought, but that experience may lead you to a new endeavor that becomes your new dream. Think of yourself as professional learner and experimenter. Your job during this transition is to try new things, whether it's something in a completely different field from your previous one, in a completely new work environment, or in a not-for-profit setting. This is a time when it's perfectly okay to fail, to discover that you're no good at one thing, or that you can't stand something else. In this way, you will discover what you are good at and what you're really driven to do.

If you don't give yourself permission to muddle around in this manner, however, the discomfort is going to bother you. Every time you try something and it doesn't work out, you're going to beat yourself up for being so dense or second guess your decision not to stay with your original career path. If you grant yourself dispensation to err, on the other hand, you'll be much more willing to explore all sorts of opportunities that come your way. You may not feel great when something doesn't work out, but you'll be better able to tolerate the discomfort and keep on trying new ventures.

• Fight mid-career inertia. This is perhaps the most crucial advice we have to offer. After working for 30 years and feeling stressed out by the last 10 years, you may start off in a new career direction, encounter some resistance, and decide it's not worth it. Instead of exploring other opportunities, you opt for mid-career drift rather than direction. If you don't have pressing financial concerns, however, you can prolong this drift indefinitely. This inert state is relatively comfortable, and even though it isn't fulfilling or meaningful, it also isn't stressful.

We're assuming that being comfortable isn't your primary mid-career goal. Don't allow inertia to stop you from pursuing the direction that you embarked on or from switching directions if that one didn't work out. Woody Allen once offered the famous advice that 80 percent of success was just showing up. We couldn't agree more. You have to keep volunteering, trying part-time jobs, starting businesses, testing jobs in different fields or sizes of companies and exploring community activities.

To help you fight the inertia that often dogs mid-career people in transition, frame each new job or volunteer experience as a potential once-in-a-lifetime opportunity that you're uniquely poised to capitalize on. Earlier we asked you to imagine the worst that might happen. Now we're asking you to imagine the best case scenario. When you hear that a local gourmet food market has an opening for a part-time salesperson, don't view this as a low-paying, nonprofessional job with no future. Instead, assuming you're interested in and have some knowledge about high-quality food, consider it a great experience if you want to open your own gourmet food shop; consider the opportunities for advancement within the store for someone with your business expertise, and think about how much you're going to learn about everything from artisanal cheeses to truffles. It may well be that a best case scenario doesn't unfold, but this attitude will get you off your rear end and in the door to find out.

LET DISCOMFORT BE YOUR GUIDE: LEE'S STORY

Having spent 25 years in managerial financial positions for large corporations, Lee enjoyed his career without loving it. He found great satisfaction in being able to provide for his family because of the good salary he received. He also relished the global travel that was part of his job and especially liked the colleagues he met and formed close relationships with over the years. When he was downsized out of a job because of a corporate staff reduction, Lee didn't miss the actual financial work as much as he did the people and the travel.

Lee embarked on the transitional phase of his career with great gusto. His passion had always been classical music—listening to it and learning about it—and he decided that he would find a second career related to this passion. He began searching for not-for-profit arts positions that would allow him to be part of the classical music world, albeit in financial roles similar to his corporate ones. Lee was fine with this compromise, but he quickly discovered that these jobs didn't pay enough—he and his wife still needed to make a certain income.

This realization created some discomfort in Lee's life, but his wife's support helped ameliorate it. She encouraged Lee to continue his search and encouraged him to work out a budget that required a specific savings amount for their retirement annually and trimmed their expenses for the next few years. Based on this budget, Lee and his wife determined that he could take a job for 50 percent less than he previously earned.

Unfortunately, none of the not-for-profit arts positions even approached that 50 percent figure. Then Lee heard about a budget analysis and planning position at a small company. The pay was a little more than half of what he made before and it only required him to work three days weekly for much of the year. The job had nothing to do with classical music, though, and both his mother and mother-in-law were appalled that he was considering part-time work "at his age." This upped the discomfort level again, and Lee questioned whether he was on the right track.

After talking with his wife and adult kids, though, Lee recognized that he could get past the stigma of working a part-time job and that the reduction in income wasn't pleasant, but he could also accept it. The key was becoming involved in the music world in some capacity. With that goal in mind, he accepted the part-time position. Within weeks, he volunteered to help at a local orchestra— he would assist in a program that introduced music to children and was in charge of bringing classes to orchestra rehearsals as well as arranging for individual performers to visit the schools. During this time, Lee told the executive director of the orchestra that he would be glad to help out in the controller's office, and his offer of help was accepted. In this way, he began gaining expertise in not-for-profit accounting practices, knowing that it would make him a good candidate for that type of job with a large orchestra.

Lee's trepidation soon melted away, and he was happy juggling his part-time job with the volunteer one, knowing that he was working his way toward a significant new career goal.

SPECIFIC SOLUTIONS FOR SPECIFIC FORMS OF DISCOMFORT

Some of you may be experiencing vague forms of unease as you make your way from one career to the next—you may know that you're fearful and fretting, but you can't identify the specific cause beyond no longer being part of a given field or company. Lee, on the other hand, recognized that money issues, an inability to find the perfect new job and the stigma of part-time work were responsible for his concerns. If you can pinpoint the cause of your malaise, you stand a much better chance of moderating it and keeping on track. To that end, let's look at some of the common causes of discomfort during mid-career transitions and the best ways to deal with them.

• *The absence of traditional job structure and predictability*. If you choose work alternatives such as a part-time position or running your own business, you may find yourself nonplussed by the lack of a familiar routine. For 30 or so years, you may have been accustomed to a nine to five day, a regular paycheck, a benefits package, annual performance reviews, and so on. Now, you feel as if you're lazy when you don't start work until ten or put in a full eight hour day; you become nervous when that paycheck doesn't arrive with regularity.

To combat this discomfort during your transition, create a formal schedule for yourself keyed to goals and time frames. Set specific objectives that you want to accomplish in the next week, month, quarter and year. Write these objectives on a piece of paper or on your computer and focus on tasks that you need to do in order to move you toward the objectives. The goals don't have to be hugely ambitious—they can be as simple as "find a volunteer position in the community," or "add one new customer for my business." The goals and the actions needed to achieve them will provide structure to your days and thus diminish your discomfort.

You should also consider paying yourself a regular salary if not receiving one bothers you. Some of our clients do this by arranging for a monthly payout of severance or a retirement lump sum. Others restructure their savings or retirement income to provide a regular payout. Remember, this payment doesn't have to go on forever; it just needs to see you through the uneasiness of your transition, which may be only a few weeks or months.

• *The lack of collegiality/camaraderie*. As part of your next step, you're going from working for a large organization to working for yourself or in a very small group. The result: You feel isolated, and it's disconcerting not to have people around to bounce ideas off of. Amazingly, you even miss the meetings.

The worst thing you can do is sit alone in your home office waiting for the phone to ring or go to a part-time or volunteer job where you have little to say to the few people in your area. Instead, join a group of like-minded individuals. Industry associations, hobbyists, online communities and cause-related groups all offer opportunities to chat about work and career issues. Depending on where you live, you may also find groups of retired executives and other people over 50 who meet regularly to discuss everything from volunteerism to small business challenges. While you may not want to become a permanent member of any of these groups, temporary membership will help you during your transition.

• *Bad manners.* When you leave a good job in a large organization to be on your own or to work for a smaller group, you may be dismayed to discover that people don't return your calls, make you wait when you have a meeting, and reply to your e-mails curtly. You may have been insulated from this lack of courtesy earlier in your career, but now in this mid-career transition phase, you're encountering it, especially if you're trying to sell yourself (to get a job), a product, or services.

As ego-deflating as these experiences may be, don't take them personally. Though we hate to encourage tolerating rudeness, we also recognize that bad business manners are often a result of time pressures and generational norms. People are so crunched for time, piling one meeting on top of another and fighting to make one deadline after the next, that they sometimes are curt out of necessity. It's also true that many younger people practice verbal shorthand when communicating online, and an e-mail that you may perceive as abrupt simply represents their norm for electronic communication.

No doubt, you will encounter some individuals who are genuinely rude and treat you as an inferior because you're trying to sell them something. As uncomfortable as these experiences are, they are the exception rather than the rule. The problem for a mid-career professional in transition mode, however, is that this exception feels like the rule when it's happening. Because you're uncertain where your new job or career is taking you, you overreact to slights. We've found that humor is often the best antiseptic for these hurts. If you can laugh at another person's superciliousness, you can take the sting out of whatever other moronic thing they say or do.

• *Rejections.* One of the nice things about being a long-time corporate employee is attaining a certain stature so that rejections are few and far between. While you may experience turn downs from bosses on projects, you generally know how to get what you want—you understand the way things work within your organizational culture and can be reasonably sure of getting people to sign off on most of your requests.

This certainty rarely exists when you go in a new career direction. Rejection is humbling, and it is part of the learning and growth process of a second career. You're going to find that some people will turn you down for jobs while others will refuse even information interviews. Rejection comes with any new territory, and you shouldn't let it get you down as you move from point A to point B.

Be aware of a pattern of rejections. For example, even though she was well into her 40s, Deborah kept being hit by the fact she didn't have a college degree. Computerized job sites eliminated her resume from consideration, search firms brought it up continually, and one prospective employer asked, "Didn't they have a tuition refund program at any of your companies?" The tipping point was a 27-year-old HR recruiter, who tossed Deborah's resume across the desk at her and said, "What's with this no college deal?" Deborah decided she wanted to put the issue to rest once and for all. She visualized herself being asked questions about her lack of a degree when she was 80. She applied to a local community college and was pleasantly surprised to find she was awarded some credits for her on-the-job learning. The day she was accepted, she was able to change the education part of her resume to "currently enrolled in degree program."

FORGE A NEW IDENTITY

At the start of this chapter, we noted that as you transition to a new workstyle and possibly a new lifestyle, you will need to create a new identity for yourself. You need to define consciously who you are in this next part of your life. By doing so, you won't feel like an imposter pretending to be a small business owner or a philanthropist.

Many ways exist to forge your new identity, but we'd like to conclude this chapter with some practical suggestions:

- Develop a fluid plan to keep you on track. As the word fluid suggests, the plan should be loosely structured and take into consideration that your plans may well change with experience. Just having a written plan, however, will give you a sense of direction, a crucial component to any new identity.
- Create business cards for yourself, even if you don't have your own business. They can say anything from "Volunteer" to "Part-Time Consultant." These cards make tangible what otherwise is only an idea in your head.
- Create a web site. Blog about your volunteering efforts and include links to sites related to your not-for-profit interests.
- Join a group of like-minded souls. We've mentioned this before, but we want to emphasize that this is a great way of establishing your new identity, especially if you're not part of an organization.
- Form your own group. Whether online or in the real world, organize people in your community (virtual or geographic) who share your interests or are mid-career people doing what you're doing.

8

Monitor Your Progress: Signs that You're Going in a Great New Direction

"**H**ow do I know that I'm doing the right thing?"

This question has many variations, and all of them relate to those moments of uncertainty that emerge when you've embarked on a new path. While some of you may be lucky and know from the start that you've made the perfect choice, others will have moments of doubt.

That's good. These moments allow you to assess whether you are on the right path, if you're on the right path but have encountered an obstacle, or if you somehow got yourself going in the wrong direction. One of the best things mid-career professionals can do as they move forward is monitor where they've been, where they are, and where they're going. In this way, they can make adjustments along the way that will keep them moving toward their new goals.

What you want to avoid at all costs is making a major mid-career change and then sticking with it blindly, even though it's not turning out as you expected. It's not uncommon for people to talk excitedly to friends and family about their new job or career, and then they can't admit to themselves or others when it isn't working out. Sometimes people are so stubborn or proud that they insist that their new job is absolutely everything they had hoped for, even when it's not. Most of the time, though, people simply are unsure if they're on the right track. Some days are great, some days are just okay, and it's difficult to know if you made the right choice. Should you try something new? Should you stick with it for another 6 months? Should you "tweak" your path to make it more compatible with what you want? By monitoring your progress toward whatever goals you've set for yourself, you can answer these questions. To that end, let's look at the key factors you should be measuring as you move forward.

MULTIPLE MEASURES

You've just made a major mid-career change. You've stopped working for a large corporation in an executive capacity and started your own consulting business. Or you shifted from the corporate sector to something completely different—you opened your own gourmet food store. Or you were working for the family business for the last 20 years and now are combining volunteering with part-time classes related to a new vocation. No doubt, as you started your new activities, you were excited, anxious and had high expectations. Over time, though, you start wondering if you made the right choice.

To assess your choice, use the following measures:

• *Financial.* This is assuming you have financial goals for your new endeavor (which you may not if your main activity is volunteer work, a hobby, travel, or spending time with the grandkids). What were your monetary objectives for your new job or business? Did you expect to make more money than you made in your previous job? Did you expect your business to be profitable within a year? Did you simply hope to make sufficient income so that you could maintain your lifestyle until retirement? Be honest with yourself in answering these questions. Don't make excuses or rationalize if you're not meeting your goals. Though making money may not be your primary goal, it is still important and some mid-career professionals want to make a certain amount of money either because they have to or for their own sense of self-achievement. If you're falling short, you should acknowledge this fact and make adjustments. If you're doing well or even better than expected, you can take this as a sign of progress.

• *Learning.* Perhaps your major goal was to acquire skill or knowledge in a new area. This can be true whether you went back to school or are learning on the job. Are you learning at the rate that you want to learn? Are you learning what you want to learn? Do you believe that the knowledge or skills you're acquiring will be as useful to you now as you thought when you started? While learning is a tougher measure to quantify than financial progress, it is also one that most people can assess with a bit of thought. Consider the most critical skill or area of information you hoped to acquire. Maybe it was learning how to run a retail establishment. Maybe you wanted to understand how to be a coach. Whatever it was, do you feel you've made significant progress toward this learning goal? Or does it seem as if you've made little or no progress and it will take far longer than you expected to achieve it?

• *Purpose.* Are your new work or non-work activities meaningful; are they more meaningful than your previous job? Do you feel as if you are making a contribution, whether to a cause, an organization, or other people? Do you have a sense that you're finally doing what you were intended to be doing? Do you go about your day feeling energized and committed? At mid-career, a sense of purpose is especially important. Before then, you may have been working for the money or doing something that you were good at and once liked, but you left it because you weren't driven to do the job anymore. Therefore, you may have made a switch designed to help you find a more meaningful activity, and you need to decide if what you're doing is providing you with that purpose. In thinking about this measure, keep in mind that purpose comes in all forms, and it can take some time before you master the skills, gain the knowledge, and become comfortable in your new role. Until that happens, you may feel like you're doing more meaningful work but fall short of Purpose with a capital P. That's fine, as long as you continue to make progress toward that goal.

• *Fun.* Are you having fun at your new job or in your new career? Is it more fun than before? Does your new enterprise or activity feel more like play than work? Does time pass quickly? Do you enjoy most of your responsibilities and tasks, and do you sometimes find yourself thinking, "I can't believe they're paying me to do this!" Don't set the bar too high for this measure. Every job or activity has its dull moments and mundane tasks. Sometimes it doesn't feel like fun when you have a great deal to learn and are under pressure to learn it. We are assuming, however, that some of you left whatever job or career you formerly had because it ceased to be fun. Many mid-career professionals talk about how something they used to love to do became drudgery, either because it had become "old" or the culture of their organizations had changed. As a result, they vowed to find something that was more fun. Consider, then, if you're having more fun at what you're now doing. Are you smiling or laughing more? Are you eager to get up in the morning and start your work? Are you finding that you're under less stress and more into the flow of things?

We recognize that these four measures are not created equal, nor should they be. For some of you, purpose may be a far more important goal than the other three. Some of you may be looking at learning as your critical objective. In these instances, achieving that particular primary goal is a better measure of how you're doing than your progress relative to the other three goals. Therefore, weigh your measure accordingly. At the same time, however, don't ignore the other three. Think about what happens when your new vocation gives you a great sense of Purpose, yet you're using old skills and learning nothing, you're not having any fun, and you're not making any money. Given this, keep all four career goals in mind, but prioritize them.

THE COMMON SIGNS OF BEING ON THE RIGHT AND WRONG PATHS

Because the middle phase of our careers often means spending time in the "muddle phase," we don't always know if what we're doing is what we should be doing. While we can be objective when writing about this phase, we know that those of you going through it are often buffeted by strong and unexpected emotions. When you've worked in one career for 30 years or for one employer for 15 years, making a switch has emotional and psychological ramifications. Your view of your new enterprise or job may be governed by feelings of revenge, a desire to show people that your dream of a new career wasn't an illusion or a need to be paid what you're really worth, and so on.

Consequently, you may start fresh and not be sure if things are going well. An objective observer may be able to say, "This is perfect for you," or "You made a mistake," but when it's happening to you, it's difficult to gain this objectivity or read the signs of progress.

To help you read the signs—both positive and negative—let's return to the common mid-career opportunities we discussed in earlier chapters and consider what might indicate progress or problems in each:

Volunteering

Some people volunteer to help those in need and discover that the experience makes them uncomfortable, but they feel guilty about admitting that the job is not for them. Other mid-career professionals believe that joining a volunteer group will be a breath of fresh air after the politics of their corporate job, only to discover that politics also exist in volunteer organizations.

Should you stay? Should you leave? Should you find a different volunteer position? We can't provide the definitive answer, but perhaps the following signs will help:

WARNING SIGNS

• *Feeling depressed, heartbroken, etc.* Dealing with disadvantaged people or those in poor health can impact different people in different ways. For some, it's too much to handle emotionally. This isn't anything to be ashamed of; we all have different tolerance levels for sad things. You may not be able to deal with seeing young kids with terrible diseases. There's nothing wrong with this, except if you persist in staying in this volunteer position and feeling sad all the time. The odds are you'll have a much greater tolerance for a different type of health or social problem, and that's where you should direct your energies.

• *Believing your skills and knowledge are being wasted.* Whether true or not, this is a bad sign. If you feel like a volunteer group is not using your abilities appropriately, you probably feel like you're wasting your time. Look for another group that will give you assignments better suited to your talents.

• *Finding yourself bored all the time.* Of course, all volunteer jobs have some boring elements, and you may find this boredom acceptable if you have responsibilities that are meaningful and rewarding. If you're bored all the time, though, you should not be a martyr to a good cause.

SIGNS OF PROGRESS

• *Receiving feedback that you're making a difference.* This feedback may come from the individuals you're helping or it may come from your colleagues or supervisors, but it suggests that you're having an impact. You may simply receive heartfelt thanks from kids you're tutoring, but you should realize that this means you're doing something right. Some people believe their volunteer efforts are futile and are frustrated all the time, but when you receive feedback that what you're doing matters, you should understand that you're making a real contribution and not take that ability lightly.

• *Transforming your work through creativity, initiative, and effort.* Some people just do what's asked of them, while others reinvent their volunteer positions. They put in more time than is required, they find more effective ways of helping others, and they come up with ideas that help the organization's staff do their jobs more effectively. This willingness to go the extra mile is a good sign that this is the right volunteer position for you.

Dee Dee is a mid-career individual who heeded these signs. At first, when she began volunteering with her church group in San Francisco on Friday nights after spending the week in her regular job as a high school guidance counselor, Dee Dee relished the experience of helping homeless people. She gained a sense of satisfaction of doing something that had a clear and immediate benefit for others, and she enjoyed the connection she forged with some of the homeless people with whom she worked. These individuals made sure Dee Dee knew that what she was doing was making a difference in their lives.

Things changed, though, when her volunteer group was taken to an area of the city populated by drug abusers. Dee Dee's church was broadening its reach, and Dee Dee was enthusiastic about part of this effort—she saw herself being able to help homeless drug addicts in the same way she was helping other homeless people. As part of the church's outreach program, a group of volunteers including Dee Dee ventured into the roughest part of the city, escorted by four former addicts who were there to make certain she and the other volunteers were safe. Dee Dee was shocked by the deteriorated physical and mental condition of the individuals she saw and met with. It was not what she had expected. She couldn't communicate with them, and she could not relate to their problems in the way she did with the homeless men and women she had helped. Fortunately, Dee Dee was aware of her emotional reaction. As much as she would have liked to do more as a volunteer, she understood that these drug addicts were in such bad shape that it was beyond her capability to try to work with them. Wisely, she stuck to her job helping homeless people where she felt valued and in synch with peoples' problems.

A New, Lower-Paying Job

Some of you are going to take jobs or opt for part-time or not-for-profit work that will pay you substantially less than you formerly earned. While you may eventually earn as much or more in your new job, you will go through a period where you're trying to get by on less. For those of you with sizable savings, this may not be a big deal. For most mid-career people, though, it can represent a serious lifestyle adjustment (not to mention a psychological adjustment).

Our client Helen, for instance, found a not-for-profit job that she loved far more than her previous corporate position, but she was paid a much lower salary. Though she recognized that she would have to be more frugal because of the lower salary, it was a shock to realize how much she needed to downsize her lifestyle. As Helen said, "I loved my new job in nonprofit, but I didn't realize how much it would bother me not to be able to go to plays and out to dinner with friends once a week or to take vacations. I managed to get my work life on track, but my social life was off track." She recognized the sign that something was amiss and considered returning to the corporate sector, but she also recognized the positive sign that her job more than compensated her for earning less money. She decided to move to a smaller, less expensive apartment, a painful decision but one that allowed her to resume many of her social activities because of the money she saved with the move.

You need to be aware how this lower salary is impacting you and your tolerance for making less. Here are the warning signs that your requirements are not being met as well as the signs of progress:

WARNING SIGNS

* *High anxiety about making ends meet.* Some people underestimate what they need to survive, and they discover that they're barely making it at their new income level. Some people can tolerate living on the financial edge and others can't. If your anxiety is too high, you need to either find a better-paying position or do as Helen did and downsize your lifestyle.

* *Poor self-esteem.* You may simply be unable to tolerate not making a six figure income or whatever you made previously. A significant percentage of mid-career professionals measured their worth at least in part by the salary they received. While some of you can leave this measure behind, others can't. If you find yourself being depressed by your drop in income, you need to do something about it rather than suffer in silence.

SIGNS OF PROGRESS

* A *sense of pride and accomplishment.* Though you can't live on pride and accomplishment, these positive feelings provide strong motivation to find a way to make ends meet. If you're feeling good about yourself despite being paid less than you're used to, that's an excellent sign.

* An *increase in pay.* This is an obvious sign of progress, but we recognize that many of you may not have been at your new career or in a new situation long enough to receive this increase. Therefore, we'd suggest evaluating as objectively as you can if you're likely to

receive additional monies based on your performance, your learning, or as you become more familiar with a new occupation or business. Have you received encouragement from your boss? Do you find yourself mastering skills and ways of operating that at first seemed foreign? Do you have a significant upside in terms of pay based on your position and your field?

A New Business Venture

It doesn't matter whether you opened a coffee shop or launched a high-tech firm with a lot of investment money behind you. If you previously worked for someone and now are operating your own company, you need to be aware if you're moving toward your new mid-career goals or are falling short. Here are the signs that will help you make this determination:

WARNING SIGNS

• *A dislike of the anxiety, stress, and uncertainty involved in being the boss.* Some people are meant to run a business and others are not. There's no way to know which one you are until you try it. It may be that you found the stress of being an employee preferable to the stress of having to make all the big decisions. If you can't sleep at night, if you've developed an ulcer or if you just don't enjoy being the person at the top, then this may not be the right direction for you.

• *An inability to rebound from failure.* Many new businesses fail. This does not deter true entrepreneurs. Resiliency is a trait that everyone who starts a business must possess. Even if your business doesn't fail, you're bound to experience some serious setbacks. If you can't handle these setbacks or start a new business if the first one doesn't work, then it may be you'd be better off working for someone else.

SIGNS OF PROGRESS

• *The business is growing.* It may not be growing by leaps and bounds, but clearly you're on to something. While it's possible to dislike running your own company even if it's doing well, growth is usually a sign that you had a good idea and are executing it with energy and creativity.

• *The decision-making responsibilities suit you.* Do you relish being the one who has to make the final decision about everything from the brand of computer you'll buy to whether you'll go into a new market? This is what many small business owners and entrepreneurs enjoy most about running their companies. They don't like being at the mercy of a higher-up who can veto their decisions and prefer both the responsibility and the risk that comes with being the boss.

Being a Consultant

Because so many of you may be considering opening a consulting firm to capitalize on your years of corporate experience, you should understand that consulting is not right for everyone. Some people love it and can't believe they didn't become consultants years ago. Others grow to hate it and can become trapped in their new roles, especially if their consulting business is doing well. After you open your consultancy and have been at it for 6 months to a year, here are some signs that will help you figure out if this was a good choice:

WARNING SIGNS

• *Difficulty dealing with clients.* If you've come from a position of influence or control, you may find client interactions irksome. Before, you were the client or customer who had others working on your behalf. Now, the tables are turned, and you find it especially problematic to fulfill a request that you disagree with. If you struggle with this issue consistently—even when you like and respect a client—then this may mean you should consider other career directions.

• *Dislike of "outsider" status.* You don't hire and direct the staff that puts your recommendations into action. You frequently aren't around to see the results of your labor—it can take months or years until your strategic recommendations are implemented and the results are in. Some people prefer insider status. They want to be in the center of the action. Consultants are often external and temporary resources, and this may not suit your personality. Recognize if the fit is poor and move on.

SIGNS OF PROGRESS

• *Relishing the role of trusted advisor.* As you gain some experience as a consultant, you may also find that certain clients rely on you for advice even more than their own people. They value your experience and expertise, and they call you before making a major move. Being a trusted advisor is flattering, not to mention financially rewarding. It may feel like the perfect role for you at mid-career.

• *Developing a niche.* Most consultants start out trying to do a variety of things, but eventually market forces move them into a niche. You may begin as a marketing consultant working on advertising, sales promotion, and public relations, but you eventually find your niche doing business-to-business advertising for family-owned companies. Developing a niche often means you've done a good job in your initial consulting assignments, word has spread about a specific area of your expertise and you are receiving referrals related to this niche. This is a sign that you have a good chance of making it in the competitive consulting world.

We should also note that during the first year of consulting, many people receive an assignment that is a crucible of sorts. They are placed in a position where they are absolutely sure of what a client should do, but the client is resisting their advice. How effectively you handle this delicate situation speaks volumes about your future as a consultant.

Our event planner Jan was in this type of situation. In fact, it occurred shortly after she left her corporate job and opened her event planning consulting business. Jan's first client was a major not-for-profit association that asked Jan to work pro-bono on their annual fundraising dinner. She agreed to the assignment so she could begin building a portfolio of clients in her new field. After meeting with the planning committee, Jean recognized that its members wanted the dinner to be a duplicate of ones held in previous years.

The executive director who had hired Jan, however, wanted the dinner to be more impactful (a major reason he had brought Jan in). When Jan mentioned this dilemma to the executive director, he backed off and said that maybe they couldn't afford the money an impactful event would cost and urged Jan to go along with the planning committee.

After her research and analysis of the situation, Jan was convinced that doing the same type of dinner was a mistake. She found herself confronting the executive director with her conviction: "You told me you wanted this dinner to be different, to be more exciting. But when I proposed something that will make it different, everyone starts worrying about costs and how it breaks with tradition. What I'm suggesting will require only incremental spending and will have a huge impact. You have to trust me and let me run with this. I won't let you down. If you want to have the dinner just as you've had it in the past, then I don't need to be involved."

This was a gutsy thing for Jan to do, especially given that this was her first consulting assignment. But right from the start, Jan sensed she had what it took to be a successful consultant, and part of this ability was drawing a line in the sand based on her expertise. The executive director decided to go with Jan's ideas, the dinner was a huge success, and she was hired to plan the dinner the following year—for a fee!

TO YOUR OWN SELF BE TRUE: BE ALERT FOR BAD FITS

Knowing yourself may seem like obvious advice, but we can't tell you the number of mid-career people who take on jobs and responsibilities that are at odds with who they are. The problem, of course, is that at mid-career we're sometimes not quite sure who we are. Having defined ourselves through a job for 20 or 30 years, we lose some of our identity when we no longer have that job or leave a chosen field. When we're confused about who we are, we can enter a new field or find an avocation that isn't really right for us. At the moment we make these choices, however, we're experimenting with new directions, which is great. What's not so great is to stay with something when it clearly is clashing with our personality, beliefs, or requirements.

For instance, many of you may discover opportunities at mid-career that look great on the surface. You enter into them with great enthusiasm, and then it becomes difficult to admit that things aren't working out. Millie, for instance, sold her business at 63 and made enough on the sale to retire. Like many professionals today, however, she had no interest in retiring. When she was asked to join a nonprofit board, not only did she accept but became the board's chairperson within a year. It seemed like the perfect position to capitalize on the business wisdom she had accumulated over the years.

In fact, it wasn't perfect. Outspoken and headstrong, Millie flourished running her own business because she was in charge; it suited who she was. As board chairperson, Millie had to deal with other board members who were as outspoken and headstrong as she was and had bigger egos to boot! To get things done, she had to cajole and lobby, activities that didn't suit her style. After a short period of time trying to be someone she was not, Millie recognized this mismatch and resigned her chairpersonship. She opted instead to remain active on the board and take charge of the finance committee, where her authoritative, no-nonsense approach was ideal for the role.

The lesson here is that when a mismatch occurs, you don't necessarily have to quit. Mid-career professionals should try to tweak their roles to suit who they are. While this tweaking isn't always possible early in a career when you lack sufficient clout, you may be in a position where an organization values you sufficiently to allow you to reshape a role for a better fit.

Another problem many mid-career professionals we've worked with have mentioned is trying to do too much too soon. We've noted that some people who have traumatic mid-career experiences suffer from inertia. Others, however, suffer from an overabundance of energy. As a result, they try to rebound from being fired or becoming bored by taking on more jobs or assignments than are good for them. Within a year after retiring from her organization, Ellen got a divorce, moved to a new apartment, began consulting, bought a dog, and started writing a book. Ellen created so much change in her life that she began to feel overwhelmed and eventually, depressed. It took her a while, but she recognized that filling her life with things to do was no substitute for finding the right mix of things.

Ellen chose to cut back and then reshuffle her activities, good advice for any of you who may be trying to do too much too soon. For a while, she cut back on the consulting and focused most of her time on going for long walks with her dog. This activity allowed her to meet other dog-walkers, who helped familiarize with her new neighborhood, including the local hospital and their need for volunteers. Ellen added a bit of volunteering to her life, which provided a good balance for her long walks. After Ellen found this good rhythm for her life, she returned to writing her book, which provided a needed outlet for the ideas she had stored from all those years of corporate work. She decided, however, to stop consulting—at least for the time being. It added too much stress to a life already filled with more than enough change.

Loneliness can also cause you to choose a job or avocation that isn't right for you. While you may have friends and family surrounding you, you feel isolated because you are no longer part of your traditional work community. Desperate to find a new group of colleagues, you may take the first job offered or become part of an organization without giving much thought to whether it suits you. We know professionals who have slogged away at unrewarding jobs just to enjoy a sense of camaraderie.

Rather than make this mistake, we suggest adopting an explorer's mentality. Don't make a commitment to a new organization right off the bat if you're not sure it's right for you. Instead, field test different experiences. Sign up for a class. Join a community organization. See if there are support groups in your area for mid-career professionals— you're likely to find some linked to your particular field or more general ones for out-of-work executives over a certain age. You might also check out web sites where you can have online discussions with peers in similar mid-career circumstances. These groups lessen the loneliness some people feel and, more importantly, they prevent rash career decisions based on this loneliness.

If you're in a good financial situation, don't feel as if you must plunge back into full-time work if that's not what you want to do. Many people we've talked to tell us that because they're "only" in their fifties or even their sixties, they are too young not to have a job. They feel guilty pursuing volunteer activities or working part-time.

Recognize that retirement isn't a sin, and that if you're ready to give up full-time work, you should do so. The only caveat is one of this book's refrains: Do something! You can grow and develop in 101 ways unrelated to full-time work. Stay in good physical condition, take computer and other types of classes, spend time reading the list of 100 greatest books, travel, do art or write, volunteer—in short, keep your mind and body active and do what you can to help others. You may discover that some combination of these non-work activities is what really excites you, and you should pursue them even if you feel too young not to work. In reality, you've reached a point in your life where you have a choice, and you should choose what works for you.

Finally, recognize that the factors that create a good fit at mid-career may not be the factors you gravitated toward when you started out. Early in a career, people tend to want to join prestigious organizations and work their way up toward perks, good salaries, and so on. Later on, though, success is often measured in broader terms. Don't discount factors such as hobbies, geography, and lifestyle issues. For many years, Kim enjoyed a dynamic public relations career in London, working for a number of agencies and then opening her own shop with a partner. The new agency was successful, but success came with a price—Kim was traveling constantly and working long, difficult hours. At first, Kim felt guilty for complaining about her work. After all, many of her friends were out of work at mid-career and she was thriving. But Kim realized that what had mattered to her earlier was no longer the driving force in her life. Yes, she liked the prestige and income her agency brought her, but it was becoming increasingly difficult for her to her enjoy her one hobby—she was a lifelong equestrienne and animal enthusiast.

Kim and her husband decided to move—to a "horsey" area outside of London. It was close enough that they could still commute to jobs (which her husband continued to do), but far enough away so they could enjoy the more rural environment they both had come to love. Though it was a difficult decision, Kim left her firm and began a business distributing homeopathic horse medicines, supplements, and grooming products. The move and new job represented a significant loss of income for Kim, and her new job was not nearly as "glamorous" as her old one. But Kim's priorities had changed. Recognizing that they had changed took a bit of time, but when she grasped that a rural environment and horse-related business were more important to her than the traditional career rewards, she was able to move forward without a second thought.

ARE YOU ON THE RIGHT TRACK; CAN YOU ANSWER THESE QUESTIONS?

Determining whether you're on the right mid-career track is not always easy for the reasons we alluded to earlier: guilt, traditional expectations, confusion, and so on. At the same time, you don't need to have the definitive answer at any one moment in time. It's quite possible that you're on the right path after you leave a job because you're bored and start your own business, but within a year or two you might start feeling burned out and be on the wrong path.

This isn't an exact science, so don't feel you must assess your progress every second of every day. Instead, every so often, take a reading of where you are and how that feels to you. Escaping your career doldrums is not just a one-time event. You may have to escape more than once. Or you may have to escape 3 years after you leave the job that burned you out rather than the moment you left it.

To take a periodic reading of how you're doing, ask yourself the following questions:

- Are you growing? Are you learning new things and meeting new people?
- Are you challenged? Do you sometimes experience some discomfort because you're tackling a project that is so new and foreign it seems scary?
- Are you happy? Do you laugh, have fun, and see the humor in your life, even when things don't go as planned?
- Do you feel good? Do you make an effort to stay fit, and are you conscious of how you appear to others, whether going to the store for a loaf of bread or out on the town?

- Do people seem to like to be around you? Do they value your ideas and energy?
- Are you giving something back to the world or to your family and friends?
- Do you have a plan for at least the next few years? Do you know what you want to accomplish or learn and have a mapped out idea of how to do it?
- Do you feel your goals are realistic and in reach? Do you believe that your activities are bringing those goals closer?
- Are you meeting your financial requirements, or are you doing what is necessary to make sure you meet them?

This isn't a questionnaire where it's okay if you get half of them right. We recognize that you might not be able to answer yes to all of them every day for the rest of your life, but if you can answer yes to all of them more often than not, than you're definitely making great mid-career progress.

9

What Next: A New 30-Year Plan

It may come as a surprise for you to learn that you may only be at the halfway mark in your career. If you're 50 and have been working in your profession for around 25 years, you may have another good 25 or 30 years left to pursue your "career." We've put that word in quotes because what you do in this second half may be different in certain respects from what you did in the first half. While some of you may continue working full-time in your chosen profession, others will change professions and work schedules, open businesses, mix in volunteering with part-time work, and embark on other new endeavors that have little to do with their first career.

All this is great if you're aware of the new possibilities. If you understand that you have another half of a career in front of you, you'll probably do some serious planning to capitalize on the opportunities that lie ahead. And if you recognize that your second career doesn't have to resemble your first, you can take advantage of a diverse range of experiences that are limited only by your interests and imagination.

We have coached many mid-career professionals who are still going strong at 65, 75, and even 85. From them we've learned some valuable lessons about what is likely to occur in this second stage. They've told us about their concerns, their challenges, and their successes. Based on these experiences, we've gathered information about what you should know as you go forward into this uncharted career territory as well as what you should do to make the most of the adventure. We'd like to share this knowledge, starting with the best ways to deal with the retirement issue when it arises.

THE R WORD: REPLACING RETIREMENT WITH RENEWAL

We've talked quite a bit about retirement, focusing on individuals who retire prematurely and find themselves bored or searching for greater meaning in their lives. If this describes you, we hope our advice has helped you unretire gracefully. But there is a larger retirement issue, one that just about all of you will face in the coming years. For whatever reason—illness, lack of energy, a wish to slow down, societal norms—you're going to consider some form of retirement. If you do decide to retire, we hope you approach it with a different mindset than generations past.

Please understand that we think it's fine if you want to follow the traditional retirement path and leave a job at age 65 or earlier, never to return. If your goals are simply to relax and do some traveling, you should try them and see if these two activities are sufficient. We suspect, however, that if you've gotten this far in the book, you probably want more.

When retirement looms in your mind or in your job, we suggest you assess it from a fresh perspective. As we've noted throughout this book, retirement means different things to different people. In a May 14, 2006 article in *The New York Times*, reporter Julie Bick used the phrase "flex retirement" to describe reduced but continuing work combined with various leisure activities. Whether you like this idea of flex retirement or have your own definition, we would urge you to stop seeing it as an end point and start looking it as a point of Renewal. Every professional, age 50 or older, can redefine and revitalize his or her career. Renewal is about reassessing your situation from numerous perspectives: financial status and requirements, health, curiosity, ambition, interpersonal relationships, geography, new interests, philanthropic drive, and so on. In the next 30 years, you may have to reassess and renew your career more than once. It's possible that retirement is the conclusion you come to after a reassessment 8 years from now; you determine that the only way you're going to escape your doldrums is by getting out of the rat race. That's perfectly okay as long as it renews your energy, your sense of purpose, and your happiness. The key, though, is thinking in terms of Renewal rather than retirement.

To that end, we ask you do the following Circle exercise. Draw a large circle on a piece of paper and divide it into eight equal pieces, with each piece representing a 3-hour segment of the weekday. Shade in four segments that represent sleep, meals, and other necessary routines of life. Shade in a fifth segment for physical activity, recreation, and fun. We've emphasized the importance of staying in shape earlier, and if you're interested in Renewal, you're going to need to be healthy to take advantage of it. Similarly, you need to allot time to enjoy yourself so you can relieve whatever stress you're under—enjoying yourself can mean anything from watching television to going fishing. This leaves us with three unshaded pieces, and here is where the real Renewal will take place. Shade each piece with a different color: blue, for example could represent the same type of work you did before; red could represent a different profession, type of work, or nature of employment (i.e. starting own business); green could be volunteerism; and yellow education (taking classes, attending seminars, learning on your own).

Divide up your color shadings based on ideal division of time. What you want to end up with is a colorful representation of what would catalyze your renewal. For some of you, all three segments will be blue. Others might have one segment yellow and green, and two other segments all red.

Now create another circle and do this same exercise based on your life 10 years ago. This time, your shaded colors represent what was your reality at that point in your life rather than what you need to renew it.

Looking at the two circles, you probably will notice a significant contrast. That's great. For most people, this contrast is the catalyst for renewal. It gives you a target to shoot for in terms of how you divide your time and activities.

We should add that you should perform this Renewal exercise annually, since it's entirely possible that you may return to the career doldrums after finding a new activity that helps you escape them. It would be great if at age 55 you turned your hobby into a business that lifted you out of the funk you were in when your former company fired you.

Recognize, though, that by age 65 you may need to shuffle the pieces and colors to lift you out of your doldrums a second time. The good news is that you may just need to do some minor tinkering. If you've been in full three-segment, red-color mode for 10 years running your hobby-business, you may just need to work one hour less each day and substitute a volunteer activity. Some of you may be ready for more leisure time combined with a less stressful, more fun part-time job.

The point is that Renewal can happen more than once, and you should use the Circle exercise to help you with this process whenever it's necessary.

THE MORE CONNECTED YOU ARE, THE BETTER YOUR NEXT 30 YEARS WILL BE

Five years from now, someone in a remote province in China may become your new company's best customer. Ten years from now, you may hear about a not-for-profit group that is ideally suited to your talents and interests. Fifteen years from now, you may learn that a former direct report has just started a business and is looking for part-time help from savvy veterans.

Staying current and connected will be more important in the second half of your career than in the first half. The world is changing rapidly, and it is no longer possible to stay current just by reading *The Wall St. Journal* or by attending an annual industry conference. Younger people may be more comfortable with technology than middle-aged professionals, but from a career standpoint, it behooves the latter group to become comfortable with it. Many of you will quickly become disconnected from what's happening in your field or from larger business and economic trends when you leave your jobs. If you're consulting, running your own business, in a small operation or working part-time, it's much more difficult to be tuned in to what's happening. When you stop having regular lunches with people in your field and attending various trade shows, seminars, and the like, you can quickly fall behind.

The Internet, e-mail, chat rooms, and other technology-related tools offer you a way to keep track of developments in your field, new business opportunities in other areas, colleagues with whom you've worked over the years, experts who can offer you advice about new ventures, groups that need volunteers with your expertise, and so on.

While most mid-career professionals we know can handle e-mail, a significant percentage don't use it much; they prefer phone calls or in-person meetings. Others have never gone into a chat room, visited a niche web site, read or created a blog, joined an online community, participated in a virtual meeting, or become skilled at searching for information and ideas through the Internet.

If you're shying away from technology in these ways, it may not hurt your career and life goals immediately, but it will almost certainly impact them at some point in the future. The world is only going to become more high-tech, not less. As difficult as it may be for you to transition to this world now, it's going to be even more difficult 5 or 10 years from now when you realize how crucial it is for whatever path you're pursuing. We strongly urge you to do whatever you must—take computer classes, get your children to teach you, experiment with the Internet on your own—to become proficient at communicating, learning, and doing business online.

If you require another motivation to be technologically with-it, consider that scores of web sites for older people have emerged, and these sites are portals for mid-career professionals interested in everything from business networking, to volunteering, to starting a business. A few years from now, you may decide you want to learn more about how you can put your years of business expertise to work for a volunteer group. Sites such as www.aarp.com, www.eons.com, www. yourencore.com, www.seniors4hire.org, and www.dinosaur-exchange. com are capable of putting you in contact with the people you want to talk to and the information you need.

Here's another incentive to become technologically proficient: You're much more likely to be hired by a company, a volunteer group, or a customer if you're skilled in this area. If you open your own business or are a consultant, prospective customers are going to expect you to have your own web site. If you apply as a volunteer or for a job at an organization, you're going to be expected to hit the ground running from a technology standpoint. If you struggle to master software, set up a video conferencing session, or raise funds online, you're not going to be as effective in your new role as you might be. Remember, too, that your supervisor in any new job, whether in the corporate or not-for-profit sector, is likely to be younger than you are and will expect and need you to be technologically savvy. A young newspaper editor was recently accused of discriminating against older workers, and he responded that they would love to hire more veteran people but that these individuals frequently had problems with the company's Mac operating system and its desktop publishing technology, preventing them from providing value immediately.

It doesn't take much time or effort to reach a level of technological proficiency, and we believe that this investment will have a higher return on investment at mid-career than just about anything you can do.

PREPARE FOR EVOLUTION: CHALLENGING CHOICES AS YOU CHANGE

Your initial escape from your career doldrums may be enormously gratifying and it may even seem as if you've found your true calling, but you should also be alert to the possibility that you may need to make some adjustments 5, 10, or 15 years from now. Fluidity and flexibility should be your guiding lights as you move forward, giving you the option to change jobs, sell a business, move to a new volunteer position, and so on. Most of you will undergo emotionally or intellectually impactful experiences in your fifties, sixties, and seventies that cause you to reassess what you're doing. As a result, you're confronted with new choices, and you should be open to making them despite all the standard excuses—being too old, too set in your routines, or too unwilling to take a risk.

The following are some common changes in circumstance and attitude that you may experience in the coming years and the choices they often catalyze.

The Impulse and Opportunity to Give Back

We've addressed how some mid-career professionals gravitate toward volunteering, but you may not be one of them, at least initially. You may escape your career doldrums by getting a new job or changing fields and be fine. Later, though, something may happen that causes you to want to spend more of your time and energy helping others. Sometimes it's the experience of becoming a grandparent and wanting to make the world a better place for your grandchildren. Sometimes it's an event that affects your life, such as visiting a third world country and witnessing the terrible poverty, or becoming ill and outraged by the health care system.

We cite these two examples because travel and interactions with the health care system tend to increase once you get past a certain age. In addition, as you become older, you're more likely to know people who volunteer, are on foundation boards and work for not-for-profits. Sooner or later, time and circumstance will place you in a position where you'll be presented with the chance to give back.

You may also accumulate sufficient funds to make giving back more feasible than it was earlier in your career. At some point down the line, you may determine that you have enough and that making money is no longer a primary goal. At that point, you may shift your focus to making a difference rather than making a buck.

Be open to these opportunities. Just because you had a plan to start your own business or to divide your time between part-time work and travel doesn't mean you can't adjust this plan. Don't resist the impulse to give because it seems at odds with what the goals you mapped out when you reached mid-career. If you are moved to work on behalf of a cause or spend your time tutoring or raising money for a local charity, heed the voice in your head urging you to change direction.

Health Crisis or Other Major Personal Problems

If you experience a personal loss or serious disease, you may find yourself in the career doldrums again. As time passes and you recover physically and emotionally, you may not regain interest in a career or any of the activities that formerly interested you. People we know who have gone through these challenging experiences note that for a while, they're uncertain what they want to do. At some point, however, they often emerge from these experiences with a clearer sense of what they want to do in the coming years, and it may be significantly different from what they had been doing.

Carol originally came to New York to pursue a dance career, and she achieved a great deal of success, becoming a soloist in the American Ballet Theater. As her career wound down, she tested other jobs to make ends meet—department store sales, health care—but discovered what she really enjoyed was the restaurant business. Carol became a part owner of a small café and moved from there to a general manager position at a well-known New York restaurant. She enjoyed the people she worked with and met as well as the responsibility.

While working at the restaurant, Carol began taking the Iyengar form of yoga classes, a highly disciplined approach. Carol loved it and took classes daily.

Then she was diagnosed with breast cancer. This was a tough period in her life, but Carol was treated successfully and returned to her job at the restaurant. The bout with cancer, though, made her think long and hard about her life and what she wanted to do with it. She realized that her true passion was yoga, and she enrolled in a year-long teacher training program. She was soon teaching as well as running the restaurant.

It was too much. Carol recognized that she had to make a choice, and it was a difficult one, since the restaurant position paid well and she was uncertain how much potential income yoga instruction might provide. Nonetheless, Carol knew that yoga was her passion and she told her bosses at the restaurant that she was leaving. They offered her more money and a more flexible schedule, but

Carol was certain that she wanted to make yoga instruction her life's work. She went about doing so with great energy and creativity, building a strong base of private clients, becoming a top yoga instructor, and teaching at a prestigious club in New York.

Today she works just as hard as she always did, but she has a totally rewarding life. She realizes that her cancer experience brought her to a place where what she could do something she loved and also make money.

Like Carol, you may find that your current mix of activities is no longer satisfying because of a personal crisis. While health-related problems are the most common cause, it may also be a late-in-life divorce or difficulties with adult children. Whatever the reason, this personal crucible may cause you to rethink what you're doing. It may make a formerly satisfying job seem meaningless. It may cause you to search for what you really love to do rather than settling for what you merely like. Though all this can engender some tough choices — Carol decided to forsake financial security in favor of what she was passionate about — it can also lead you toward an enormously satisfying new career or life path.

Relocation

This is the time in your life when you may decide to move to a warm weather climate or another city to be closer to your adult children and grandchildren. You may also move because you've always dreamed of living in a certain part of the country and now you have the money and freedom to act on that dream.

When you relocate, you invariably open yourself up to a new group of people and experiences. You're exposed to ideas and information that start you thinking about your work and your future in different ways. You may meet someone who coaches little league and asks you to assist him or her, or a person who works with the disabled and suggests you could volunteer to do the same thing. The new geography may also spawn new interests. If you move to a place with beautiful forests and wild regions, you may become a hiker. If you move to a place near a large body of water, you may learn to be a sailor or fisherman. Or you may learn to make a living doing something in synch with your new surroundings—becoming a guide, for instance.

Psychologically, too, relocation puts you in a new frame of mind. If you recently retired and had decided to do a bit of consulting, play golf, and not do much else, relocating may alter this plan. You may be re-energized by your move and determine to go back to full-time work. You may discover that you have huge opportunities in a smaller market (if that's where you relocate to), and that your experiences with a big company in a big city make you a valuable commodity in your new location.

Be prepared for these choices when you relocate. Though it's possible that a new location can initially cause you to feel out of place (figuratively, not just literally), and you may struggle from a career standpoint for a while, it also can provide you with a fresh start. Don't rule out trying something new when you relocate. Be open to the people, jobs, and volunteer opportunities that come your way.

Discovering a New Hobby or Interest

When you reach age 50 or 60, you often have more time on your hands than earlier in your life when your career was all-consuming and your children demanded a great deal of your time and energy. With more time, you have greater opportunities to explore new hobbies, take classes in subjects that interest you, and so on. Though it may not happen when you first enter the mid-career doldrums, somewhere down the line you'll find that you have the time and the inclination to pursue an avocation or leisure time activity. You may also learn as you're pursuing it, that it gives you far greater satisfaction than the job you held for the last 25 years.

Should you turn that woodworking hobby into a full-time business? Is it possible that you might be able to make good money selling your collection of art pottery online? Are your new photography skills at a level that you might start charging people money for your work and turn photography into a profession? If you love coaching kids at soccer, might you go back to school, get a degree, and try to find a coaching job with a school?

Before answering these questions, make sure you can do so objectively. Some mid-career people think they're not entitled to turn a newly discovered mid-career hobby or interest into a full-time business or profession. They tell themselves that "it's just a hobby," and that making anything else out of it is a pipedream.

Perhaps. But it's entirely possible that this hobby is what they've been searching for in a profession all their lives. We've seen people retire or burnout from traditional professional careers, go through a period of readjustment, and then start filling their time with a hobby or taking classes. Before they know it, this leisure time activity becomes their passion.

If this happens to you, don't dismiss it. You may be one of those lucky individuals who stumble upon a true calling later in life and have the chance to make a decent living from it for the next 20 years.

Given the number of choices these four kinds of life changes can engender, what should you do? Many mid-career professionals tell us that they don't want to change jobs or careers at the first sign of dissatisfaction, especially after they already emerged from mid-career doldrums and thought they had found a good path for themselves. They don't want to act impulsively and give up what might be the best mixture of activities for them just because something changes in their lives.

To help you know if you're just being impulsive or if you should make new choices, use the following steps to evaluate your decision:

1. Consider the risk-reward scenario for making the choice to change. Determine how much you're risking financially versus how much you stand to gain, either financially or in terms of meaningful, purposeful activities.

2. Assess how powerful your impulse is to redirect your career and life. On a scale of 1 to 10, is it in the 7 to 10 range? Put another way, if you had to measure your motivation to redirect your activities, would you term it moderate, significant, or overwhelming?

3. Note how much time has passed since one of the four evolutionary events we just described occurred. If relatively little time has passed (a week, a month), then it's likely you're being impulsive.

If two or three months or more have elapsed, you've probably given your decision some serious thought.

4. Project the outcome of your decision to change direction. Think about whether it will help you achieve a new career or life goal, such as doing work that you're passionate about, contributing to a worthwhile cause, or gaining knowledge.

5. Do a reality check by estimating the odds of your endeavor giving you what you want. Create odds for a very specific outcome (i.e. turning a hobby into a full-time, profitable business). Are the odds reasonable or is it a long shot?

These five steps can be used at any point in the future. We've found that many mid-career professionals make at least one additional career or activities change after they make their first one. Frequently, a significant period of time goes by between this first and second change. At age 53, they may decide to retire from one job and go back to school. At age 58, they may use their new degree to enter a different profession. At age 64, they may switch to part-time in order to devote more time to a cause with which they've become involved.

Therefore, use these five steps to test your decision whenever it occurs.

IF YOU NEED HELP DOWN THE ROAD . . .

Because of our backgrounds, we are biased in favor of coaching for mid-career professionals. Nonetheless, we strongly believe this bias is justified. Mid-careerists often go through not just one but multiple transitions. As challenging as an earlier career transition might be—such as moving from subordinate to a managerial role or taking on a global assignment—it often pales in comparison with mid-career shifts. Not only are mid-career professionals often dealing with huge changes in their lives, such as moving from one profession to another type of work, but they also must overcome the inertia and confusion that can emerge at mid-career.

They also must evaluate new and sometimes unfamiliar opportunities. Some people at mid-career have more options than they know what to do with. They may have the financial freedom to arrange their lives 10 different ways, and as wonderful as that is, it also helps to have guidance to figure out the single best way. Coaches can offer advice about the pros and cons of a job change, a career shift, the implications of taking a part-time position, and the possibilities of re-educating oneself for a future career. Most of all, they are someone to turn to one, two, or three years down the road when work or life throws you a curve and you're not sure how to handle it.

Some have called coaches business or career therapists, and that's an apt term. They can be a sounding board for your ideas and give you objective feedback when you're trying to come to terms with a new challenge. A good coach can also help you create a plan for the next 5 years—not a blue sky plan but with clear action steps and measurements. This coach can also provide you with a useful assessment of your experience and expertise, suggesting what options your background makes realistic and which ones aren't feasible. In short, a wise coach helps you see your range of options and evaluate them astutely.

Exhaustive lists (literally hundreds of thousands) exist on the web for finding coaches. Be as specific as possible when searching (e.g., "coaches with banking expertise in northern New Jersey"). There are also web sites for groups like the International Coaching Federation and others that pinpoint specific coaches. The Yellow Pages and personal referrals are other sources. In fact, if you start asking friends and colleagues about coaches, you'll be surprised at how many of them have worked with these professional advisors. Be aware, though, that coaches tend to specialize and find niches. Some work strictly online and by phone. We would encourage you to find coaches who favor face-to-face contact—personal meetings combined with phone sessions are usually effective. Most coaches will offer a complimentary session and we highly recommend taking advantage of this offer. While you're not going to be miraculously cured of your mid-career doldrums during an initial meeting, you should be able to determine if you have good chemistry with a coach, as well as his or her coaching process.

THRIVING IN CHANGING TIMES: HOW TO ROLL WITH THE PUNCHES AND MAKE THE MOST OF OPPORTUNITIES

We have no doubt that as much as society and business have changed in recent years, the pace of change will be even swifter in the coming years. Dramatic change tends to present the most opportunities to those individuals with skills, contacts, savvy, and a good financial base. In other words, most mid-career professionals are in an excellent position to capitalize on whatever trends emerge. To capitalize on them, it really doesn't matter if your mid-career path involves becoming an entrepreneur or an employee, a part-time worker or a volunteer (or any combination of these pursuits). You're going to have more options than you ever had before, primarily because you've accumulated the resources that younger, less experienced people lack.

In fact, a number of trends unfolding today suggest that even more opportunities for mid-careerists will exist in the future. Aging baby boomers are a huge market, spurring the growth of fields such as money management, estate management, health care and alternative medicine, eldercare, travel, and so on. In many instances, this market wants to be served by people their own age. They want doctors and therapists who they can identify with, they want financial planners who are old enough to understand the issues they're facing, and they prefer travel agents who grasp the types of trips they're interested in taking.

Perhaps the most significant trend of all, though, is that this aging baby boomer generation is changing the way people think about work and age. We've already discussed how baby boomers are redefining what retirement means and when it takes place. More that that, though, is the sense that people can start over at age 50, 60, 70, or 80; that it is perfectly reasonable to expect a 53-year-old former corporate executive to open a restaurant or for a 62-year-old lawyer to return to school to obtain a teaching certificate. The baby boom generation has also made it clear that starting fresh doesn't have to involve a traditional move to a new job, but can involve a mix of untraditional activities—from volunteering to part-time work to re-education. The notion of infinite possibilities is fast becoming the norm for mid-career professionals who have sufficient resources to consider multiple options.

Of course, 25 more years of infinite possibilities comes with its challenges, not the least of which is choosing from among these possibilities. It also means moving past the boredom and burnout that can hit people in mid-career, overcoming the inertia and low self esteem that can strike when you've been fired, or discovering that retirement wasn't what you expected.

Still, we have every confidence that you can overcome these obstacles and meet the challenges that you'll encounter in the coming years. We're confident because we've seen many other mid-career professionals achieve incredible things in their second and third careers. And we're confident because we believe in the advice we've offered throughout this book and know that it can facilitate your journey.

Of all the advice, perhaps the single most important suggestion is to be positive and adaptable. All sorts of opportunities are going to arise, but it's likely that at least some of them will be opportunities in areas other than your chosen, professional field. Be open-minded, be willing to learn, and be ready to try something new if it represents something you're passionate about. If you adopt this attitude, you will quickly emerge from your mid-career doldrums and discover enriching, meaningful experiences that equal or surpass anything that came before.

Appendix 1

Financial Issues to Consider When Changing Jobs or Careers

By Brendan T. O'Connor, CFP

You've worked at the same company for 10, 20, or even 30 years, and you wake up one day and you are no longer employed . . . It could be because the company is downsizing, your job goes overseas, or you decide to change careers. This can be a trying time because your financial future is no longer predictable, or worse—you could experience financial difficulties.

If you are not presently working with a Certified Financial Planner (CFP®) you should consider hiring one to create a financial plan. This plan should show a projection of your income and expenses, and will be helpful in determining several things:

1. Whether you can you maintain your present lifestyle with a lower paying job.
2. If you don't get another job or you begin a new career how long you can maintain your lifestyle.
3. If you can retire now, maintain your lifestyle, and not run out of money.

Whether you work with a CFP or if you decide to do it yourself, the following items can help you to deal with this situation more smoothly:

CASH FLOW—"LIVING EXPENSES"

It is very important to know what you are spending to maintain your lifestyle. This spending is known as "living expenses." In order to maintain your lifestyle during a job or career change, you need to be able to generate enough income to cover living expenses. As tedious as it may be, you should take the time to summarize your monthly and yearly expenses. Do not include income taxes or payroll taxes because these are not living expenses. You should know how much you will need when you have no wages, salary, bonus, etc.

CASH FLOW—"EMERGENCY FUND" VS. INCOME

It is advisable to have an "emergency fund" to help maintain your lifestyle in tough times, which may be when you are changing jobs or careers. The fund should be approximately 3 to 6 months of living expenses. For example, if you spend $120,000 per year, then you will need $30,000 to $60,000 in the fund. Another source of money for the emergency fund is a home equity credit line, which you can access by writing checks. But, be careful of using a home equity credit line for two reasons: (1) you will incur an additional cost (i.e., interest expense), and (2) the interest rate can increase substantially.

When the emergency fund runs out you may need to generate income from investments (interest and dividends), proceeds from selling investments, and even distributions from retirement assets (see the following section). The income tax consequences of these income sources may vary significantly, so you should discuss these options with your tax advisor. Make sure your advisor works with you to avoid any penalties from premature distributions from retirement assets.

RETIREMENT ASSETS/OTHER ASSETS

It is usually advisable to maximize contributions to your retirement assets, especially when a company match is involved. This is one of the best ways to accumulate assets to be able to retire and maintain your lifestyle, or to provide income if you lose or change your job.

Here are some of the more common retirement assets: 401(k) Plan, Profit Sharing Plan, Defined Benefit Plan, and IRAs. You may also have other assets that you may be entitled to or have accumulated as an employee, such as stock options, deferred compensation, vacation pay, severance pay, etc.

When your employment ends, you should find out all of the assets and accounts you are entitled to and request current balances. Then, you should determine your alternatives regarding these assets, such as:

- Can you keep monies in the company retirement plan(s)?
- Must you transfer the assets out of the retirement plan(s)? If so, when?
- When must you exercise options?
- Is the pension available as a lump-sum?

You may want to "rollover" the retirement assets into your own IRA.

MEDICAL/HEALTH INSURANCE

If you were covered under your employer sponsored policy, will you be covered after your employment ends? If so, for how long? Check with your employer. Your coverage may be continued under the Consolidated Omnibus Budget Reconciliation Act (COBRA). COBRA provides terminated employees the option to continue coverage under the former employer's policy for up to 18 months.

Determine if a new employer has a medical or health insurance plan. If not, look into obtaining coverage personally. Be prepared, because it won't be cheap.

OTHER ISSUES

- Notify your former employer of any changes in mailing addresses, phone numbers, etc.
- Obtain and document dates when you are entitled to retirement benefits, or when you must take distributions from retirement assets.
- Determine if you are entitled to unemployment compensation. If so, apply as soon as possible.

- If you participate in a group life insurance plan, determine if you can continue. You may be able to convert from a group-term to a permanent insurance policy. But note that this converted policy may be more expensive than buying a new policy if you are in good health.
- Are you covered under a disability insurance policy? Consider a personally owned disability insurance policy.

In the final analysis, if you are more knowledgeable about your financial situation you will be better able to adapt during this challenging time.

Appendix 2

13 Step Networking Process

1. Ask your contact to pave the way with a telephone call or note.

2. Prepare what you want to communicate during your initial contact (but don't recite it as if you were reading from a script):

- Who referred you
- Specific information/advice you're seeking
- Your request for 20 to 30 minutes of talk time.

3. Call early mornings, mid-week, avoiding Monday, Fridays, and late afternoons. Request specific days and times for meetings (specificity increases the odds of people agreeing to see you).

4. Focus on the present and not the past during this initial call:

- Don't rehash past job experiences.
- Talk about what's happening in their organization or their industry now.
- Send them your resume at the end of the conversation only if it is requested.

5. Seek information during the meeting but also view it as a potential link to another meeting; ask for other referrals.

6. Follow up the meeting with a short thank-you note that includes:

- a reference to a key point made during the meeting
- a stated next step that allows you to remain in contact with this person ("Ill check back with you in two weeks to let you know how my meeting goes with your friend.")

7. Keep detailed, organized records, summarizing what took place during the meeting and next steps.

8. Purge stale names as you expand your networking contacts.

9. Prioritize new leads that emerge from a meeting over lukewarm ones from earlier meetings.

10. Determine timing of referrals:

- Clarify if you should call contacts directly or if your contact would prefer to speak to them first.
- Call contacts in a timely manner, especially when someone has gone out of his or her way to help you.

11. Be organized; keep written notes about your growing list of contacts and "to do" actions regarding each.

12. Be persistent without being obnoxious. Follow up with calls and notes (or e-mails) when appropriate.

13. Schedule networking as a daily activity; the more you do it, the more likely it is to pay off.

Appendix 3

Business Plan Outline

These are the factors you need to consider before starting a new business or a consulting practice.

Description of business or consulting initiative
- Product/service features and benefits

Competitive analysis
- Industry profile
- Direct competition
- Indirect competition
- What differentiates your business from competition

Financial plan
- Cost of start-up
- Ongoing operating costs
- Sales and income projections
- Estimated return on investment in first and second year
- Sources of financing

Legal issues
- Trademarks, patents, copyrights, licenses
- Product/service liability

Marketing plan
- Target market analysis
- Customer profile
- Pricing
- Customer service
- Advertising and promotion
- Publicity/media relations
- Web site

Management
- Board of directors/advisory board
- Management team
- Recruitment of employees
- Employee compensation

Operations
- Distribution
- Facilities
- Suppliers

Projected financial statements
- Monthly cash flow report
- Monthly income statement
- Monthly balance sheet

Appendix 4

Employment Opportunities on the Internet

The following is a list of the web sites recommended by Mullin & Associates, Ltd. You can get more information about career transitions by visiting www.mullinassociates.com. We should note that these sites are just a very small sampling of what exists online. We offer them as starting points only, not as a comprehensive resource.

ACADEMIC/EDUCATION

Academic Employment Network—www.academploy.com
> Paid site. $19.95 for 6 months access to database of K-12 employment opportunities.

Jobhunt—www.job-hunt.org/academia.shtml
> Wide ranging source of jobs and resources in the academic/education space, including placement, networking, and advice. Information is for both K-12 and higher education.

Chronicle of Higher Education—www.chronicle.merit.edu—update to www.chronicle.com/jobs/
> News and advice, CV/resume development, and job postings. Information on salaries and compensation. Very useful site for people in the academic community.

ACCOUNTING/BANKING/FINANCE

American Banker—www.americanbanker.com
Primarily a professional news and information web site.

American Institute of Certified Public Accountants—www.aicpa.org
Main site for CPAs. Career resources include job and resume postings and online classifieds. A useful resource for candidates in the CPA field.

Jobs for Bankers Online—www.bankjobs.com
175 jobs across the United States online at the time of this writing. Jobs range from teller to CFO.

Securities and Exchange Commission—www.sec.gov
Useful for accessing financial filings on public companies.

Wall Street Journal—www.careers.wsj.com
Career Journal has extensive resources for the job seeker, including job searches and resume posting. Articles on trends in particular sectors (notably financial). Much more in depth than most other sites.

DIVERSITY

Advancing Women Homepage—www.advancingwomen.com
Site provides resume and job postings. Also links to advice on career strategies, networking, and workplace communication.

EOP Publications—www.eop.com
This site allows candidates to submit resumes to a database accessible by advertisers of EOP magazines (e.g., Equal Opportunity Magazine, African-American Career World Magazine). Sponsors career fairs throughout the country.

Hispanstar—www.hispanstar.com, www.hispanicbusiness.com
The home page for Hispanic Business magazine, this is a very good web site devoted to business and general news for Hispanic Americans.

ENGINEERING

American Society for Engineering Education—www.asee.org
> A society for educators in engineering and their supporters. There are no dedicated career resources, but the society has frequent conferences that can serve as networking opportunities.

Engineering Jobs—www.engineeringjobs.com
> A simple useful site for engineers to post resumes, find recruiters and smaller employers, and search for societies and other resources.

IEEE Job Bank—www.ieee.org
> The web site for the Institute of Electrical and Electronics Engineers has extensive resources for job seekers and employers. Employment Navigator collects 5 million job leads from 160,000 web sites and places them in a single searchable database for members.

IEEE Computer Society—www.computer.org
> Career resources here link to the IEEE's job site.

ENVIRONMENT

Environmental Careers Organization—www.eco.org
> The career portion of the site contains extensive information regarding the types of careers and salaries in this space. There are also links to the largest environmental consulting firms and other resources.

FOOD/CHEFS/HOSPITALITY

Escoffier Online—www.escoffier.com
> Web site for culinary professionals. Job postings are through chefjobsnetwork.com.

Star Chefs—www.starchefs.com
> The web site is a resource for culinary professionals to discuss many different aspects of the business. There are approximately 200 jobs posted on the site and members can post resumes. The career center provides advice on the mechanics of the job search and includes an "ask the expert" section as well.

GENERAL EMPLOYMENT

Occupational Outlook Handbook—www.bls.gov

The web site is for the Bureau of Labor Statistics with a link to the OOH. The OOH provides detailed descriptions of hundreds of occupations, including necessary training and qualifications, job outlook, earnings, related occupations and sources of additional information. This information is especially relevant for candidates looking to make a career transition.

Benefits Link—www.benefitslink.com

This site is tailored towards employee benefits for professionals, including a job board. The site could also be useful for candidates looking for further information on ERISA and other employee benefits.

Career Magazine—www.careermag.com

A generalized job and resume posting web site. There are numerous postings listed and career resources available.

Career Builder—www.careerbuilder.com

A very extensive web site with many thousands of postings from both employers and executive recruiters. Career resources are available. This site should be a regular stop for all types of job seekers.

Hot Jobs—www.hotjobs.com

Provided by Yahoo! Extensive job listings, but a very large percentage of them are by executive search firms. May be useful to identify the types of assignments recruiters are working as well as individual positions

Infospace—www.infospace.com

Infospace is a yellow pages/white pages directory. A useful resource for directions and looking up phone numbers and addresses, but not directly related to the job search.

Job Banks USA—www.jobbankusa.com

Resume and job posting resources. The site also presents an extensive list of typical interview questions and advice on how to answer them.

Monster—www.monster.com

Monster is a premier career search web site. It contains detailed job postings with excellent sorting and filtering capabilities. The site also provides considerable career advice, interview strategies, and the like. This site is a must for anyone in the job market.

NYSDOL Home Page—www.labor.state.ny.us

The web site has a large number of job postings and information on companies in New York State. While this site may not be an obvious place for candidates to uncover job opportunities, it is useful. The www.hightechny.com affiliate site is very useful for those in IT, engineering, architecture, and other technically oriented industries.

GOVERNMENT JOBS

Federal Gateway—www.firstgov.gov

The federal government's official web portal. The government jobs link on the page includes extensive information on government jobs, including the application procedure and job postings at various agencies. This is a valuable first resource for individuals looking for employment by federal or state governments.

New York City Jobs—www.nyc.gov

Under the Government heading "Working for NYC" there are links to the various agencies hiring.

GRAPHIC ARTS

Creative Freelancers Online—www.illustratorsonline.com

Provides very basic job postings, pricing guides for freelance work, and advice for the freelancer.

HR

SHRM Online—www.shrm.org

Society for Human Resource Management. Numerous job postings are available for those in the human resources job category as well as career and job search advice. This site is particularly valuable for HR personnel of all kinds.

INFORMATION TECHNOLOGY

Computer Works — www.computerwork.com

Numerous detailed job postings with compensation figures. Jobs are permanent, consulting, and contract. Excellent career resources. Resume posting and detailed job search abilities. Highly recommended for IT professionals.

Computer Jobs — www.computerjobs.com

Extensive job postings can be broken out by specialty, software, platform, etc. Resume posting (including security clearances) and a section for consultants to create a personal profile online. Also has generalized career resources. Recommended for the IT consultant.

Dice — Resources from IT Recruiters — www.dice.com

Large number of job postings from both recruiters and employers, both contract and permanent. Articles related to IT employment and trends. Resume posting, including security clearances. Recommended site.

Job Circle — www.jobcircle.com

Regional job directory for the Middle Atlantic States. Numerous jobs in technology, but the site is not specifically dedicated to IT. Generalized career resources, job, and resume postings.

Just Tech Jobs — www.justtechjobs.com

Funnels users to specific areas based on skill set (C++, Cisco, etc.) Site allows for resume posting and job search. A number of jobs are posted.

LEGAL

American Bar Association — www.abanet.org

A critical site for all attorneys. There is a section for ABA sponsored career advancement and networking opportunities.

Attorney Find — www.attorneyfind.com

Web site allows potential clients to identify attorneys geographically and with necessary expertise. Could be useful for an attorney to network with others in a desired location and field.

Attorney Jobs Bulletin—www.attorneyjobs.com
Subscription based site with thousands of jobs nationally for attorneys.

MAGAZINES

Businessweek—www.businessweek.com

Forbes—www.forbes.com

Fortune—www.fortune.com

Harvard Business Review—www.harvardbusinessonline.com
All of these magazines and their web sites are essential tools for anyone in business or seeking employment. While none has a page dedicated to job postings, *Business Week* has a section with some particularly insightful articles on career advice and job hunting. *Fortune's* jobs section is hosted by CareerBuilder. Neither the HBR nor *Forbes* have career sections, but *Forbes* does have a CEO Network section, where senior executives can exchange ideas and chat with *Forbes* senior editors. This feature requires verification as a CEO.

ENTREPRENEURIAL

Inc.—www.inc.com
A vital resource for entrepreneurs. Nothing specific for the job search, but another good resource for job hunters seeking new and growing firms. There is a section dedicated to HR management of the entrepreneurial firm.

MEDICAL PROFESSION

Bio—www.bio.com
A web site for the life science research community.

Physician's Employment—www.physemp.com
Employment site for physicians. No resume posting. Many jobs listed, many by recruiters. Useful web site for physicians seeking employment, especially in hospitals.

NEWSPAPERS

NYT on the Web—www.nytimes.com
> Job Market section has excellent articles on job searches of various types. Extensive postings of jobs and resume posting.

Wall Street Journal—www.wsj.com
> Essential reading for the business executive.

NEWSWIRES

Businesswire—www.businesswire.com
> Source of breaking news releases and regulatory filings for companies around the world. Free registration required for full text access. Very useful for monitoring releases of targeted companies.

PR Newswire—www.prnewswire.com
> Press releases from news and business. Primarily oriented towards journalists, but helpful for others as well.

NOT-FOR-PROFIT

Chronicle of Higher Education—www.chronicle.com/jobs
> Job search, research, and up-to-date articles concerning the field of Higher Education.

Philanthropy News Digest—www.foundationcenter.org/pnd
> Daily updated news site regarding fundraising and establishing a foundation.

Idealist.org—www.idealist.org
> A project from Action Without Borders. Search over 60,000 nonprofit organizations in 135 countries. Contains a large section of job postings within these companies.

Nonprofit Oyster – www.nonprofitoyster.com
> Nonprofit job search site connecting employers and candidates.

RESEARCH

Bookwire—www.bookwire.com
> Leading site for general information and news on the book publishing industry. Recommended for candidates researching the publishing industry.

Hoover's Company Profiles—www.hoovers.com
> Part of Dunn and Bradstreet. Fee based, with some company background information available free.

SEC Edgar Archives—http://sec.gov/edgar.shtml
> Online repository for registration statements, periodic reports, and other forms with the SEC. Primary source for financial statements.

SCIENCES

Bi-On-Line (Bio.com)—www.bio.com
> Exists as an online community of scientists, professionals, businesses, and organizations supporting the life sciences for the purpose of facilitating communications and disseminating information within that community.

Medsearch America—www.medsearch.com
> Part of Monster.com, specifically for healthcare.

Pharmaceutical Online—www.pharmaceuticalonline.com
> Web site dedicated to the pharmaceutical manufacturing industry. Information for pharmaceutical professionals. Jobsearch provided by VertMarkets.

Science Online—www.sciencemag.org
> Web site for *Science* magazine and the American Association for the Advancement of Science. Wide range of articles across all disciplines. Good career resources for scientists and a number of global jobs posted.

SALES/SALES MANAGEMENT & MARKETING/ADVERTISING

Advertising Age—www.adage.com
> Vital reading for the sales and advertising executive. Job listings in the Career Center at the bottom of the page.

Brandweek Online Welcome—www.brandweek.com
> Extensive news articles on corporate marketing. Part of the VNU EMEDIA group, partnered with *Adweek, Mediaweek, VNU News,* and *Editor & Publisher*. Highly recommended. Job search and posting through *Adweek*.

Marketing Jobs—www.marketingjobs.com
> Extensive job listings for sales and marketing around the country. Links to free industry magazines, job, and resume postings. Recommended at minimum as an industry research resources.

SELF EMPLOYMENT

Be the Boss Top Franchise Opportunities—www.betheboss.com
> Directory of franchising opportunities with industry publications. Searchable by industry and initial investment. Resource for individuals considering starting their own business under a franchise or franchising out their own business.

CNN Money – www.money.cnn.com
> Essential financial and business site, with sections on small business.

WIBO—www.wibo.org
> Workshop in Business Opportunities. "Boot camp" for entrepreneurs. Resources for entrepreneurs to be successful.

The Franchise Handbook: Online—www.franchise1.com
> Directory of franchising opportunities

U.S. Business Advisor—www.smartbiz.com
> Internet technology for startups and small business. Information on business strategies. Relevant for entrepreneurs and start ups looking to leverage the Internet.

U.S. Small Business Administration—www.sbaonline.sba.gov
> Essential resource for small businesses and people looking to work for themselves. Extensive resources on business planning, financial assistance, counseling, regulation, and compliance.

VOLUNTEERING

Volunteer Groups—www.networkforgood.org, www.volunteermatch.org, or www.idealist.org.

These three sites are representative of the thousands of volunteer-related sites you'll find online when you do a search using the word, volunteer. You can also sort by cause, such as "volunteer arts," or "volunteer cancer; " or by organization, such as "United Way volunteers," or "Salvation Army volunteers;" or by location, such as "volunteer California," or "volunteer abroad."

Index